Learn German (Prepare for DELF A1.1) (German Edition)

A Simple Guide for Beginners

Multibhashi Pvt. Ltd.

pencil

ISBN 978-93-5610-049-7

Published in India 2022 by Pencil

A brand of
One Point Six Technologies Pvt. Ltd.
123, Building J2, Shram Seva Premises,
Wadala Truck Terminal, Wadala (E)
Mumbai 400037, Maharashtra, INDIA
E connect@thepencilapp.com
W www.thepencilapp.com

Author biography

Multibhashi

Office no 214, Second floor, Arcade, Brigade Metropolis, Mahad- evapura, Bengaluru, Karnataka 560048
www.multibhashi.com

Note:

In a few lessons we have added QR codes which contains youtube videos.

Please follow below steps:

1. To scan QR code go to : www.qrcodescan.in
2. Select "allow" option to scan
3. Click on "Open" to play videos

CONTENTS

German Basics

OBJECTIVE: To get familiar with the language and learn the German alphabet.

Concept A: Introduction to the language and the country.

- Widely spoken in Germany, Austria, and Switzerland.

- **Famous places in Germany.**

- **Food items and drinks**

- **Oktoberfest in Munich**

Concept B: Purpose of learning German

- **German**is the second most commonly used scientific language.

- It makes you creative (**Germans are innovators.**)

- It is not a very hard language and hence it is very easy to learn it.
- To explore new things and learn with fun.
- Also learning a new language gives one a new and global perspective.

Concept C: Alphabets and their pronunciations (including special cases)

German Alphabets					
Aa ah	Ää Ah Umlaut	Bb beh	SS ess-testt	Cc tseh	Dd deh
Ee eh	Ff eff	Gg geh	Hh Ha	Ii ee	Jj yot

Kk kah	Ll ell	Mm emm	Nn enn	Oo oh	Öö Oh Umlaut
Pp peh	Qq kuh	Rr err	Ss ess	Tt teh	Uu uh
Üü Uh Umlaut	Vv fow	Ww veh	Xx ks	Yy upsilon	Zz tsett

Concept D: German constant with sound, examples, and meaning in English.

Constant	Sound	German Word	Meaning
SS	ss	heißen	To be called
ei	ai	nein	no
ie	ee	nie	never
st	sht	stuhl	chair
sp	shp	spiel	game
J	Y	ja	yes
V	F	voll	full
ich	ish	ich	I

uch	ookh	buch	book
ä	ae	hände	hands
ö	eo	hören	hear
ü	eu	tür	door

Eu----oy

Eg: Euro

·ig---ish

Eg: fertig (finish)

(To understand pronunciation)

(Auf Deutsch)

Zum Beispiel- example

Eg: Wasser (water)

Explanation: a= aa , e=a

Concept D: Phonetics

• Repeat the pronunciation of the words after the trainer and learn examples.

Practice A: Spell your name using the German alphabet.

(Buchstabieren Sie ihr Name bitte)

i.e. Spell your name, please.

- PRAKASH

Practice B: Spell the other persons' (your family members, friends, trainer, etc…) first name and last name.

- SHARON
- LOBO

Answers to Practice A:

- PRAKASH

peh err aah kah aah ess ha

Answers to Practice B:

- Vorname- First Name

  SHARON

  Ess ha aah err oh enn

- Nachname- Lastname

  LOBO

  ell oh beh oh

AUF WIEDERSEHEN!!!! (See you again) OR TSCHÜSS(Bye)

Scan the QR code to play the audio

Pronunciation Practice:

ah	a
bay	b
tsay	c
day	d
ay	e
eff	f
gay	g
hah	h
yot	j

kah	k
ell	l
em	m
en	n
on	o
pay	p
koo	q
er	r
es	s
tay	t
ooh	u
fow	v
vay	w
ix	x
ih	y
tset	z
ä	e in melon
ö	i in girl
ü	u in dude
ß	ss

heißen	To be called
nein	no
nie	never
stuhl	chair
spiel	game
ja	yes
voll	full
ich	I
buch	book
hände	hands
hören	hear
tür	door

German Greetings and Essentials

GREETINGS, YES AND NO, PLEASE AND THANK YOU — THE BARE MINIMUM YOU NEED TO SURVIVE!

Objective: To learn the Formal and informal greetings

Concept A: Formal Greetings

- **Guten Morgen**- Good morning

- **Guten Tag**- Good day/ Good afternoon
- **Guten Abend**- Good evening
- **Gute Nacht**- Good night
- **Hallo**- Hello
- **Wie geht es Ihnen?**- How are you (Formal) : Ihnen is the appropriate formal address for a stranger, especially someone older, and people in positions of authority.
- **Entschuldigen Sie Bitte:**Excuse me Please
- **Willkommen**: Welcome

Saying goodbye in formal way :

Auf Wiedersehen (OWF vee-der-zey-hen) : You have probably heard “Auf Wiedersehen” before. It literally means “until we see each other again”.

Concept B: Informal Greetings

- **Hey**- hey
- **Hi**- Hi
- **Bis bald**- See you soon
- **Bis später**- See you Later
- **Bis dann**- See you then
- **Bis Morgen**- See you Tomorrow

- **Bis Freitag**- See you on Friday

- **Wie geht es dir?**- How are you (Informal) : Use dir when speaking to someone young or someone you know very well.

- **Wie geht's?**: Similar to wie geht es dir, but more casual. This essentially translates to "What's happening?" or "How's it going?" (Geht's is a shortened form of geht es, so Wie geht's? literally means "How goes it?")

- **Gut, danke.**: Good, Thanks

- **Mir geht es Gut, danke**: I am Fine, thanks.

- **Es geht:**So So

- **Mir geht es Schlecht:**I am not doing well

- **Mir geht es Besser:**I am doing better

- **Viel Spaß! :**This means "Have fun!" and can be used in many conversational contexts—for example, when saying goodbye to friends who are going to a party, on a trip, etc.

- Once you've said that you're fine, or good, or so-so, it is customary to ask how the other person is doing. You can do this easily by saying **und dir**? (And you? [Informal]) or **Und Ihnen**? (And you? [Formal]).

<u>Saying GoodBye in a Casual Way:</u>

Tschüss (cheus)- Bye

Concept C:"Please" "Sorry" and "Thank you"

You never know how long you're going to be stuck with Jens in this imaginary island scenario, so it's best to be polite. For that, you're going to need these words:

- **Bitte:**Please
- **Danke schön:**Thank you
- **Danke:**Thanks
- **Entschuldigung**: Excuse me
- **Es Tut mir Leid**: I am sorry
- **Ja:**Yes
- **Nein:**No
- **Vielleicht:**May be
- **Alles Gute:**All the Best
- **Viel Glück:**Good Luck

Practice A : Formal : How do we say the following in German:

1. Good Morning
2. Good Afternoon

3. Good Evening
4. Good Night
5. Hello
6. How are you? (Formal)

Practice B : Informal : How do we say the following in German:

1. Hi
2. Bye
3. See you Later
4. See you Tomorrow
5. See you Soon

Finde bitte die Kokosnüsse

It's good to know how to sound polite during a conversation. However, after a few days on the island, Jens might not be around to converse with if he doesn't learn some survival skills…fast!

Answers for Practice A:

1. Guten Morgen
2. Guten Tag
3. Guten Abend
4. Gute Nacht
5. Hallo
6. Wie geht es Ihnen?

Answers for Practice B:

1. Hi
2. Tschüss
3. Bis später
4. Bis morgen
5. Bis bald

Scan the QR code to play the audio

Pronunciation Practice:

Guten Morgen	Good morning
Hallo	Hello
Guten Tag	Good day/ Good afternoon
Guten Abend	Good evening
Gute Nacht	Good night
Auf Wiedersehen	GoodBye
Entschuldigung	Excuse me
Es Tut mir Leid	I am sorry
Bitte	Please
Ja	Yes
Wie geht es Ihnen?	How are you?
Willkommen	Welcome
Entschuldigung Sie Bitte	Excuse me Please
Wie geht es dir?	How are you?(informal)
Hey	Hey
Hi	Hi
Bis bald	See you soon

Bis später	See you Later
Bis dann	See you then
Bis Morgen	See you Tomorrow
Bis Freitag	See you on Friday
Wie geht's?	How's it going?
Gut, danke.	Good, Thanks
Mir geht es Gut,danke	I am Fine, thanks.
Es Geht	So So
Mir geht es Schlecht	I am not doing well
Mir geht es Besser	I am doing better
Viel Spaß!	Have fun!
Und dir?	And you? [Informal]
Und Ihnen?	And you? [Formal]
Nein	No
Tschüss, (choos)	Bye
Danke schön	Thank you
Danke	Thanks
Vielleicht	May be
Alles Gute	All the best
Viel Glück	Good Luck

Short Self Introduction

Objective:I should be able to introduce myself in German confidently.

Remember:

- 'Sie' means 'formal'
- 'Du' means 'informal'

Concept A: Introduce yourself and ask the other person his/her name.

Expressions:

- My name is ____.
- I am ____.
- What is your name?

(Auf Deutsch)

- Was ist dein Name?
- Mein Name ist ____?

Or

- Ich heiße ____.

Concept B: Talk about your age and birthdate and ask the other person too.

Expressions:

- How old are you?
- I am __ years old.
- When is your birthday?
- My birthday is on___.

(Auf Deutsch)

- Wie alt bist du?
- Ich bin ___ Jahre alt.
- Wann ist dein Geburtstag?
- Mein Geburtstag ist am dritte(3rd) Februar.

Concept C: Tell where you are from i.e. your city/town and ask the other person too. Also, tell me about where you live currently.

Expressions:

- Where are you from?
- I belong to__
- Where do you live?
- I live in ____

(Auf Deutsch)

- Woher Kommen Sie? / Woher kommst du?
- Ich komme aus Indien.
- Wo wohnen Sie?/ wo wohnst du?
- Ich wohne in Pune

Concept D: Ask the trainees about the languages they are familiar with and also share your views

Expressions:

- Which languages do you speak?
- I speak ____

(Auf Deutsch)

- Welche Sprachen sprechen Sie?
- Ich spreche English, Hindi, Marathi und Deutsch.

Concept E: Discuss your hobbies and ask them what they love doing in their free time.

Expressions:

- Was sind deine Hobbys?
- Meine Hobbys sind_____ (more than one)
- Mein Hobby ist ___. (only one)

Practice A: Answer the following questions about yourself:

1. What is your name?
2. Where are you from?
3. How old are you/ What is your date of birth?
4. Where do you live?
5. Which languages do you speak?
6. What are your hobbies?

Practice B: Use the above taught sentences to give a 4-5 line short introduction of yourself.

Answers Practice A:

1. Mein Name ist _____
2. Ich komme aus ______
3. Ich bin ____ Jahre alt
4. Ich wohne in ___
5. Ich spreche _____
6. Meine Hobbies sind ______ (OR) Mein Hobby ist ____

Answers to Practice B:

1. Mein Name ist Sharon.
2. Ich komme aus Indien.
3. Ich bin zwanzig (20) Jahre alt.
4. Ich wohne in Pune.
5. Ich spreche english, hindi, marathi and deutsch.
6. Mein hobby ist tanzen.

Scan the QR code to play the audio

🔊 Pronunciation Practice:

Sie	formal
Du	informal
Was ist dein Name?	What is your name?
Mein Name ist____	My name is __
Ich bin____	I am ___
Mein Name ist____	My name is __
Ich bin____	I am ___

Wie alt bist du?	How old are you?
Ich bin ___ Jahre alt.	I am __ years old .
Wann ist dein Geburtstag?	When is your birthday?
Mein Geburtstag ist am 3rd February.	My birthday is on___
Woher Kommen Sie? / Woher kommst du?	Where are you from?
Ich komme aus Indien.	Where are you from?
Ich komme aus Indien.	I belong to__
Wo wohnen Sie?/ Wo wohnst du?	Where do you live?
Ich wohne in Pune	I live in ____
Welche sprachen sprechen Sie?	Which languages do you speak?
Ich spreche English, Hindi, Marathi und Deutsch.	I speak ____
Was ist dein hobbies?	What is your hobbies?
Meine Hobbies sind_____ (more than one)	My hobbies are _____
Mein Hobby ist ___. (only one)	My hobby is _____

Grammer Basics

Objective:I will be able to understand the basics of grammar.

Concept A: Sentences

(sentences-Sätze)

1. For sentences:

   SUBJECT + VERB + ...

   Verb should take the second position

Example: I like to travel.

(Auf Deutsch)

Ich reise gern

- Ich = I
- reisen= travel
- gern= like

Example:- Ich lese Buch nicht gern

- Ich= I
- lesen= read
- nicht= not
- gern= like

Common verbs used

- schwimmen – to swim
- spielen- to play
- tanzen – to dance
- singen – to sing
- kochen – to cook
- backen – to bake
- gehen – to go
- kommen – to come
- studieren – to study
- machen – to do
- fahren/ reisen – to travel
- schlafen – to sleep

Concept B: Questions (frage)

- There ARE TWO TYPES of questions.

- Yes/no (Satzfrage)
- Brief answer (W – Frage)

1. **Satzfrage:**It is also called Ja/Nein Frage, because the answer requires Ja/Nein i.e. confirmation is required in the answer. It starts with the verb itself.

For questions:

VERB + SUBJECT + …..

Verb should be at the first position

Example:- Do you like to cook?

Kochen Sie gern?

- Kochen = to cook
- Sie = you (formal)
- Gern = like

Example:- Do you understand German?

Verstehen Sie Deutsch?

- Verstehen = to understand
- Sie = you (formal)
- Deutsch = German

2. **W – Frage:**It is called W – Frage because all the words start with W. Some information is required in the answer.

- Wer - who
- was - what
- wen - whom (Akk)
- wie - how
- wem - whom (Dat)
- wann - when
- wo - where
- warum - why
- woher - where from
- wesse- whose
- wohin - where (to)
- welche- which
- wie viel - how much
- wie viele- how many
- wie weit - how far
- wie lange- how long

Example:-

- Wer ist die Lehrerin?
- Wie studieren Sie?

- Was kaufen Sie?

Concept D:ARTICLES-(ARTIKELS)

Articles are modifiers especially used before a noun in a sentence. It helps clarify the meaning of the noun in a sentence. There are two types of articles- Definite and Indefinite articles. Definite article comprises 'the' and indefinite articles comprise of 'a'(and its variation 'an' when used with words starting with vowels). In German, the articles are divided according to the cases, i.e. Nominative, Accusative and Dative, respectively. Also in German, each noun has a gender. So the articles are divided according to gender, and are assigned to each noun according to its gender.

1. Nominative is the case used for a sentence, where the noun or pronoun is the subject.
2. Accusative is the case which shows the relationship between the direct object and the verb. It answers the question 'Wen'(who/whom) and 'Was'(what).
3. Dative is the case which shows the indirect object of the verb. The indirect object of the verb is the recipient of the direct object. It answers the question 'Wem'(to whom) and 'Was'(what).

	M	**F**	**N**	**Plural**
Nominative	der	die	das	die

	ein, kein	eine, keine	ein, kein	keine
Accusative	den	die	das	die
	einen, keinen	eine, keine	ein, kein	keine
Dative	dem	der	dem	den+n(while writing plural, we add an 'n' at the end)
	einem, keinem	einer, keiner	einem, keinem	keinen+n

*In German we add an article 'kein', which means 'not'.

Example-

1. Das Hausist klein. (The house is small)- Here the 'Haus' is the subject and therefore the case is nominative and the article used is 'das' as the 'haus' is neuter gender.

2. Ich schreibe den Brief.(I am writing the letter)- Here letter is the direct object, on which the action is happening, and therefore the case is accusative, and the article used is 'den' as 'Brief' is masculine gender.

Note

1. Subject can either be a noun or pronoun.

2. All nouns in German have an aNote: rticle and the article is always placed BEFORE the noun

TIP: When you ask 'what' question based on the verb, you should get OBJECT as the answer.

Example:-

1. Wir sehen ein Spiel im(in dem) Stadion (das)
2. Sie kaufen eine Tasse (die)
3. Ich habe einen Hund (der) und eine Katze (die)
4. Wie backen Sie einen Kuche ?(der)
5. Ich esse einen Apfel(der)

v **For a person:**

- Wer ist das?
- Das ist Peter.

Note: You should always ask the question WHO to get the answer.

v **For a thing:**

- Was ist das?
- Das ist ein Bus.

Note: You should always ask the question WHAT to get the answer.

FOR SINGULAR:

Example:-

- Der Apfel ist rot.

  (i.e) the apple is red

- Die Katze ist freundlich.

  (i.e)the cat is friendly.

- Das Auto ist teuer.

  (i.e) the car is expensive.

NOTE: For plural, in the nominative case, the article for all plural nouns is DIE

Concept E:PRONOUNS

Nominative:

- ich- I

- Du- you (informal)
- er - he
- wir- we
- es - it
- sie - she
- Sie - you (formal)
- Sie - they
- Ihr - you all
- father: der Vater
- mother: die Mutter
- brother: der Bruder
- sister: die Schwester
- house: das Haus
- book: das Buch
- Notebook: das Heft
- car: das Auto

HOW TO RECOGNIZE GENDER IN GERMAN

DER

All masculine gender.

Example:- Der Mann, Der Lehrer, Jahreszeit (season), Tage/ Monate (days/ months)

Words ending with …ling, …ant, …us, ...ich/ig

Example:-

- Schmetterling (butterfly)
- Elefant (elephant)
- Zirkus (circus)
- Teppich (carpet)

DIE

All feminine gender.

Example:- Der Frau, Die Lehrerin

Words ending with …ei, …schaft, …heit/keit, …ung, ….tat, …ion, …ik, …ie, …ur

Example :-

- Bibliothek - library
- Freundschaft - friendship

- Gesundheit - health
- Schwierigkeit - difficulty
- Landung - landing
- Universität - university
- Situation - situation
- Logik - logic
- Biologie - biology
- Kultur - culture

DAS

Words ending with …chen, …um, …ment, ….ma.

Example:-

- Mädchen - girl
- Museum - museum
- Experiment - experiment
- Thema - topic

Where do we apply capital letters in German?

1. First letter of the first word of the sentence.(Just like English)
2. All the Nouns (position in the sentence is immaterial)
3. "Sie" and the words associated with "Sie"(Ihnen – Ihr – Ihren – Ihrem –Ihres – Ihre – Ihrer)

1. Der Mann ist Arzt.
2. Ist Ihr Bruder Arzt?
3. Sie hilft Ihnen.

Practice A: Translate the following sentences into German.

1. I like to dance.
2. I do not like to sleep.
3. I do not like to study.
4. I like to play.

Practice B: Using the previous sentences form questions in German.

Example:

1. I like to cook.
2. Do you like to cook?

Practice C: From the below sentences classify the article as Masculine, Feminine, Neutrum

1. Der Computer ist sehr alt
2. Die Tasche ist blau.
3. Das Zimmer ist groß.
4. Die Flasche ist neu.
5. Das Hemd ist schön.
6. Der Hund ist nicht so gut.
7. Der Mann ist glücklich.
8. Die Frau ist freundlich.

Answers to Practice A:

1. Ich tanze gern.
2. Ich schlafe nicht gern.
3. Ich studiere nicht gern.

4. Ich spiele gern.

Answers to Practice B:

Sentence:- Ich koche gern.

Question:- Kochen Sie gern?

1. Ich tanze gern.- Tanzt du gern?/ Tanzen Sie gern?
2. Ich schlafe nicht gern.- Schläfst du gern?/ Schlafen Sie gern?
3. Ich studiere nicht gern.- Studierst du gern?/ Studieren Sie gern?
4. Ich spiele gern.- Spielst du gern?/ Spielen Sie gern?

Answers to Practice C:

Masculine	**Feminine**	**Neutrum**
Der Computer	Die Tasche	Das Zimmer
Der Mann	Die Flasche	Das Hemd
Der Hund	Die Frau	

Scan the QR code to play the audio

Pronunciation Practice:

sätze	sentences
Ich	I
reisen	travel
gern	like
lesen	read
nicht	not
schwimmen	to swim
tanzen	to dance

spielen	to play
singen	to sing
kochen	to cook
backen	to bake
kommen	to come
gehen	to go
studieren	to study
machen	to do
fahren	to travel
schlafen	to sleep
Sie	you (formal)
Deutsch	German
W Frage	W-Questions
was	what
wer	who
Verstehen	to understand
wie	how
wen	whom (Akk)
wann	when
wem	whom(Dat)

warum	why
wo	where
wesse	whose
woher	where from
welche_	which
wohin	where (to)
wie viele	how many
wie viel	how much
wie weit	how far
wie lange	how long
Artikles	Articles
Priya ist Arm.	Priya is poor.
Das Haus ist klein.	The House is small
Der Apfel ist rot	the apple is red
Die Katze ist freundlich.	the cat is friendly.
Das Auto ist teuer.	the car is expensive.
Auf Deutsch	in German
Du	you (informal)
er	he
wir	we

es	it
sie	she
Sie	you (formal)
sie	they
Ihr	you all
die	the (feminine)
der	of the
das	the
ein	an
einen	one
Wer ist die Lehrerin?	Who is the teacher?
Wie studieren Sie?	How do you study?
Was kaufen Sie?	What are you buying?
Wir sehen das Spiel in Stadion	We see that game in the stadium
Sie kaufen die Tasse	You buy the cup
Ich habe der Hund und die Katze	I have that dog and that cat
Wie backen Sie der Kuche ?	How do you bake the cake?
Ich esse der Apfel	I eat the apple

Wer ist das?	Who is this?
Das ist Peter.	This is Peter.
Was ist das?	What's this?
Das ist ein Bus.	It's a bus.

Days of the Week and Months of the Year

objective: To be able to learn the days and months and also pronounce correctly.

Concept A: Discuss the days of the week

ENGLISH	DEUTSCH	PRONUNCIATION
Monday	Montag	Mon—taag
Tuesday	Dienstag	Deens-taag
Wednesday	Mittwoch	Mitt-wokh
Thursday	Donnerstag	Don-nahs-taag
Friday	Freitag	Fry-taag
Saturday	Samstag	Zams-taag
Sunday	Sonntag	Zon-taag

Concept B: Discuss months of the year and also which season takes place in which month

ENGLISH	DEUTSCH	PRONUNCIATION
January	Januar	Yaa—nuuu---aar
February	Februar	Fay—bruuu—aar
March	März	Mae--erts
April	April	aa-preel
May	Mai	Maa—ee
June	Juni	Yuuu—neee
July	Juli	Yuuu—leee
August	August	Aaoo-- goost
September	September	Zep-tem-ber
October	Oktober	Oc-to-ber
November	November	No-fem-ber
December	Dezember	Dec-tsem-ber

Concept C: Discuss the seasons and also which month falls under which season

- SOMMER- SUMMER

  Juni to August

- HERBST- AUTUMN

  September to November

- WINTER- WINTER

  Dezember to Februar

- Frühling- SPRING

  März to Mai

Practice A: Given below are names of months in English, give their German names.

1. February
2. June
3. August

Practice B: Given below are names of days of week in English, give their German names.

1. Monday
2. Saturday
3. Friday

Role Play A: On telling the name of the season, the trainee will tell all months that fall under that season.

Answer to Practice A:

1. Februar
2. Juni
3. August

Answer to Practice B:

1. Montag
2. Samstag
3. Freitag

Scan the QR code to play the audio

Pronunciation Practice:

Montag	Monday
Dienstag	Tuesday
Mittwoch	Wednesday
Donnerstag	Thursday
Freitag	Friday
Samstag	Saturday
Sonntag	Sunday

Januar	January
Februar	February
März	March
April	April
Mai	May
Juni	June
Juli	July
August	August
September	September
Oktober	October
November	November
Dezember	December
SOMMER	SUMMER
HERBST	AUTUMN
WINTER	WINTER
Fruhling	SPRING

German Numbers (Cardinal and Ordinal)

Objective: To Discuss the Cardinal and Ordinal Numbers

Concept A: Cardinal and Ordinal Numbers

Numeral	Cardinal	Ordinal	Pronunciation	Numeric Form
1	eins	erste	EHR-ste	1
2	zwei	zweite	TSVEY-te	2
3	drei	dritte	DRIT-te	3
4	vier	vierte	FEAR-te	4
5	fünf	fünfte	FUHNF-te	5
6	sechs	sechste	ZEX-te	6
7	sieben	siebte	ZEEB-te	7
8	acht	achte	AHKT-te	8
9	neun	neunte	NOIN-te	9

10	zehn	zehnte	TSAYN-te	10
11	elf	elfte	ELF-te	11
12	zwölf	zwölfte	TSVOLF-te	12
13	dreizehn	dreizehnte	DRY-tsain-te	13
14	vierzehn	vierzehnte	FEAR-tsain-te	14
15	fünfzehn	fünfzehnte	FUHNF-tsain-te	15
16	sechzehn	sechzehnte	ZEX-tsain-te	16
17	siebzehn	siebzehnte	ZEEB-tsain-te	17
18	achtzehn	achtzehnte	AHKT-tsain-te	18
19	neunzehn	neunzehnte	NOIN-tsain-te	19
20	zwanzig	zwanzigste	TSVAN-tsig-ste	20
21	einundzwanzig	einundzwanzigste	EYN-und-tswan-tsig-ste	21
22	zweiundzwanzig	zweiundzwanzigste	TSVEY-und-TSVAN-tsig-ste	22
23	dreiundzwanzig	zweiundzwanzigste	DREI-und-TSVAN-tsig-	23

			ste	
24	vierundzwanzig	vierundzwanzigste	FEAR-und-TSVAN-tsig-ste	24
25	fünfundzwanzig	fünfundzwanzigst e	FUHNF-und-TSVAN-tsig-ste	25
26	sechsundzwanzi g	sechsundzwanzigs te	ZEX-und-TSVAN-tsig-ste	26
27	siebenundzwan zig	siebenundzwanzig ste	ZEEB-und-TSVAN-tsig-ste	27
28	achtundzwanzig	achtundzwanzigst e	AHKT-und-TSVAN-tsig-ste	28
29	neunundzwanzi g	neunundzwanzigst e	NOIN-und-TSVAN-tsig-ste	29
30	dreißig	dreißigste	DRY-tsig-ste	30
40	vierzig	vierzigste	FEAR-tsig-ste	40
50	fünfzig	fünfzigste	FUHNF-tsig-ste	50
60	sechzig	sechzigste	ZEX-tsig-ste	60
70	siebzig	siebzigste	ZEEB-tsig-	70

			ste	
80	achtzig	achtzigste	AHKT-tsig-ste	80
90	neunzig	neunzigste	NOIN-tsig-ste	90
100	(ein)hundert	(ein)hundertste	Eyen-Hundher-ste	100

Practice Questions A: Cardinal and Ordinal Numbers:

1. One and First :
2. Two and Second :
3. Three and Third :
4. Four and Fourth :
5. Five and Fifth :
6. Six and Sixth :
7. Seven and Seventh :
8. Eight and Eighth:
9. Nine and Ninth:
10. Ten and Tenth:
11. Eleven and Eleventh:
12. Twelve and Twelfth:
13. Thirteen and Thirteenth:
14. Fourteen and Fourteenth :
15. Fifteen and Fifteenth :
16. Sixteen and Sixteenth :
17. Seventeen and Seventeenth :
18. Eighteen and Eighteenth :
19. Nineteen Nineteenth :

20. Twenty and Twentieth:

Practice B

1. Her family has three houses. ? Cardinal or Ordinal ?
2. Did Virat Kohli make the 20th Century ? Cardinal or Ordinal ?
3. He has two daughters. Cardinal or Ordinal ?
4. They live on Tenth Floor ? Cardinal or Ordinal ?

Answers to Practice question A

1. Eins und Erste
2. Zwei und zweite
3. Drei und dritte
4. Vier und Vierte
5. fünf und fünfte
6. Sechs und Sechste
7. Sieben und Siebte
8. Acht und Achte
9. Neun und Neunte
10. Zehn und Zehnte
11. Elf und Elfte

12. Zwölf und Zwölfte
13. Dreizehn und Dreizehnte
14. Vierzehn und Vierzehnte
15. fünfzehn und fünfzehnte
16. Sechzehn und Sechzehnte
17. Siebzehn und Siebzehnte
18. Achtzehn und Achtzehnte
19. Neunzehn und Neunzehnte
20. Zwanzig und Zwanzigste

Answers to Practice question B

1. Cardinal
2. Ordinal
3. Cardinal
4. Ordinal

Scan the QR code to play the audio

Pronunciation Practice:

eins	1
zwei	2
drei	3
vier	4
fünf	5
sechs	6
sieben	7
acht	8

neun	9
zehn	10
elf	11
zwölf	12
dreizehn	13
vierzehn	14
fünfzehn	15
sechzehn	16
siebzehn	17
achtzehn	18
neunzehn	19
zwanzig	20
einundzwanzig	21
zweiundzwanzig	22
dreiundzwanzig	23
vierundzwanzig	24
fünfundzwanzig	25
sechsundzwanzig	26
siebundzwanzig	27
achtundzwanzig	28

neunundzwanzig	29
dreißig	30
vierzig	40
fünfzig	50
sechzig	60
siebzig	70
achtzig	80
neunzig	90
(ein)hundert	100
erste	1
zweite	2
dritte	3
vierte	4
fünfte	5
sechste	6
siebte	7
achte	8
neunte	9
zehnte	10
elfte	11

zwölfte	12
dreizehnte	13
vierzehnte	14
fünfzehnte	15
sechzehnte	16
siebzehnte	17
achtzehnte	18
neunzehnte	19
zwanzigste	20
einundzwanzigste	21
zweiundzwanzigste	22
zweiundzwanzigste	23
vierundzwanzigste	24
fünfundzwanzigste	25
sechsundzwanzigste	26
siebundzwanzigste	27
achtsundzwanzigste	28
neunundzwanzigste	29
dreißigste	30
vierzigste	40

fünfzigste	50
sechzigste	60
siebzigste	70
achtzigste	80
neunzigste	90
(ein)hundertste	100

Review 1

Objective: To revise the topics which we have done in the previous days

Concept A: German Greetings

We have formal and informal greetings in German language.

If we are talking to unknown strangers, elderly people, customers etc, we use formal greetings

If we are talking to known people, friends, family etc, we use informal greetings.

Let us go through all the greetings both formal and informal.

- 'Sie' means formal.
- 'Du' means informal.

Formal Greetings

- **Guten Morgen**- Good morning
- **Guten Tag**- Good day/ good afternoon

- **Guten Abend**- Good evening
- **Gute Nacht**- Good night
- **Hallo**- hello
- **Wie geht es Ihnen?**- How are you (Formal) : Ihnen is the appropriate formal address for a stranger, especially someone older, and people in positions of authority.
- **Entschuldigen Sie Bitte:**Excuse me Please
- **Willkommen** : Welcome

Saying Goodbye in formal Way :

- **Auf Wiedersehen (OWF vee-der-zey-hen)**: You have probably heard "Auf Wiedersehen" before. It literally means "until we see each other again".

Informal Greetings :

- **Hey**- hey
- **Hi**- hi
- **Bis bald**- See you soon
- **Bis später**- See you Later
- **Bis dann**- See you then
- **Bis Morgen**- See you Tomorrow

- **Bis Freitag**- See you on Friday
- **Wie geht es dir?**- How are you (Informal) : Use dir when speaking to someone young or someone you know very well.
- **Wie geht's?**: Similar to wie geht es dir, but more casual. This essentially translates to "What's happening?" or "How's it going?" (Geht's is a shortened form of geht es, so Wie geht's? Literally means "How goes it?")
- **Gut, danke.**: Good, Thanks
- **Mir geht es Gut, danke**: I am Fine, thanks.
- **Es geht**: So So
- **Mir geht es Schlecht**: I am not doing well
- **Mir geht es Besser**: I am doing better
- **Viel Spaß!**: This means "Have fun!" and can be used in many conversational contexts—for example, when saying goodbye to friends who are going to a party, on a trip, etc.
- Once you've said that you're fine, or good, or so-so, it is customary to ask how the other person is doing. You can do this easily by saying **Und dir?**(And you? [Informal]) or **und Ihnen?**(And you? [Formal]).

Saying goodBye in a Casual Way:

- Tschüss, (cheus) - Bye

Concept B: Alphabets:

In the German language, the alphabet has 26 letters, 3 umlauts (Ä, Ö, Ü) and one ligature (ß). Some letters are pronounced very similar to the English pronunciation, but some others are a little different. Just listen many times to the German letters and the sounds will become familiar. Also, don't get confused by our special letters **ä, ö, ü and ß.**

A, B, C, D, E, F, G, H, I, J, K, L, M, N, O, P, Q, R, S, T, U, V, W, X, Y, Z, Ä, Ö, Ü, ß

Concept C: Numbers

- 1: eins
- 2: zwei
- 3: drei
- 4: vier
- 5: fünf
- 6: sechs
- 7: sieben
- 8: acht
- 9: neun
- 10: zehn
- 11: elf

- 12: zwölf
- 13: dreizehn
- 14: vierzehn
- 15: fünfzehn
- 16: sechzehn
- 17: siebzehn
- 18: achtzehn
- 19: neunzehn
- 20: zwanzig
- 21: einundzwanzig
- 22: zweiundzwanzig
- 23: dreiundzwanzig
- 24: vierundzwanzig
- 25: fünfundzwanzig
- 26: sechsundzwanzig
- 27: siebenundzwanzig
- 28: achtundzwanzig
- 29: neunundzwanzig
- 30: dreißig

As you all now know how to say numbers till 30. Let us follow the same process we followed from 21 to 30 for the remaining numbers

Let's all say all the numbers together

Concept D: Self introduction

Do a short self introduction of yourself in German language which should cover the below points:

1. Was ist Ihr Name?
2. Was sind Sie von Beruf?
3. Wie alt sind Sie?
4. Wo wohnen Sie?
5. Was sind Ihre Hobbys?

Concept E : Days and months of the year

Quickly list out the days and months in German which you have learnt:

- Januar (yah-noo-ahr) - January
- Februar (fay-broo-ahr) - February

- März (mehrtz) - March
- April (ah-pril) - April
- Mai (my) - May
- Juni (yoo-nee) - June
- Juli (yoo-lee) - July
- August (ow-goost) - August
- September (zehp-tehm-ber) - September
- Oktober (ok-toh-ber) - October
- November (no-vehm-ber) - November
- Dezember (de-tsem-ber) - December

Concept F: Time in German

- Die Zeit : Time
- Die Uhr: Clock

You can use the following phrases as a guide when talking about time and dates in German:

- **Wissen Sie, wie viel Uhr es ist?**(Do you know what time it is?)
- **Wie viel Uhr ist es?**(What time is it?)
- **Haben Sie ein paar Minuten Zeit?**(Do you have a couple of minutes to spare?)

- **Um wie viel Uhr fahren Sie ab?**(What time do you leave?)
- **Es ist früh.**(It's early.)
- **Du kommst aber spät.**(You're really late.)
- **Welchen Tag haben wir heute?**(What day is today?)
- **Heute ist Freitag.**(Today is Friday.)
- **Der Wievielte ist heute?**(What's today's date?)
- **Heute ist der dritte Mai.**(Today is the third of May.)
- **Alarm**: Der Alarm
- **Alarm Ruf:**Alarm call

Vocabulary for telling time in German:

- ***Uhr***– The German equivalent of o'clock, used to denominate full hours.
- ***Um***– Means as in "Let's meet at four o'clock".
- ***vor***– Before like in "Seven minutes before midnight".
- ***nach***– The antonym of vor, of course meaning after.
- ***viertel***– This means quarter like in quarter past/quarter to.
- ***halb***– meaning half and is used to denote the half hour intervals between full hours. More on this below.

Practice A:

Please tell the below in German language:

1. 12:30
2. 13:40
3. 4:15
4. 9:00

Practice B:

Please tell the below numbers in German language:

1. 12
2. 67
3. 90
4. 36
5. 120
6. 234

Practice C:

Please tell the below in German language:

1. March
2. August

3. June

4. May

ROLE PLAY A:

Initiate a conversation with your partner and ask about the following points:

1. Name

2. Beruf

3. Alter

4. Handynummer/Telefonnummer

5. Hobbies

6. Birthday

ROLE PLAY B:

Do the following below.

1. Bitte buchstabieren Ihre Name (Spell out your name please)

2. Say all the days of the week in german

3. Say all the months of the year according to the below seasons given:

   Winter

   Sommer

Herbst

Autumn

Frühling

ROLE PLAY C:

Ask random questions on the below given points.

1. The pronunciation of alphabets
2. Numbers
3. Months and days
4. Greetings
5. Time

Answer to Practice A:

1. 12:30 : halb eins
2. 13:40: dreizehn Uhr vierzig minuten
3. 4:15 : viertel nach vier
4. 9:00: neun Uhr

Answer to Practice B: Please tell the below numbers in German language:

1. 12 : zwölf
2. 67 : siebenundsechzig
3. 90 : neunzig
4. 36: sechsunddreizig
5. 120: einhundertzwanzig
6. 234: zweihundertvierunddreizig

Answer to Practice C: Please tell the below in German language:

1. March : März
2. August: August
3. June: Juni
4. May: Mai

My Family

Objective : To discuss the German's Verb to have (haben) and its conjugation and Discussion about My family

Concept A : "Haben" - To have

German	English
ich habe	I have
du hast	You have
er hat sie hat es hat	he has she has it has
wir haben	we have
ihr habt	you (guys) have
sie haben	they have
Sie haben	you have

Regular Conjugation : The below explanation is about Regular Conjugation:

- Ich -e
- du -st
- er/sie/es -t
- Wir -en-n
- Ihr -t
- sie/Sie -en -n

Concept B: Implementation of Verb "haben" in the Sentences

- I have a Father: Ich habe einen Vater.
- You(Informal) have a Sister : Du hast eine Schwester.
- He has a lot of Brothers: Er hat viele Brüder.
- She has a Daughter : Sie hat eine Tochter.
- It has many questions : Es hat viele Fragen.
- We have a Son : Wir haben einen Sohn.
- You all have a Family: Ihr habt eine Familie.
- They have a Grandmother : Sie haben eine Großmutter / Oma.

- You (Formal) have a Grandfather : Sie haben einen Großvater/ Opa.

Concept C: My Family (Meine Familie)

- mother die Mutter
- sister lie Schwester
- cousin die Cousine
- father der Vater
- brother der Bruder
- cousin der Cousin
- son der Sohn
- aunt die Tante
- niece die Nichte
- daughter die Tochter
- uncle der Onkel
- nephew der neffe

Practice A: Conjugate the verb "Haben" according to the subject.

1. I have a Brother: Ich ...

2. You have a Sister: Du ...

3. He has a Grandfather: Er ...

4. She has a Grandmother: Sie …

5. It has a nice question: Es …

6. We have an Uncle: Wir …

7. You all have an Aunt: Ihr …

8. They have a Niece: Sie ...

9. You (Formal) have a Nephew: Sie ...

Practice B: About Our Family

1. Uncle :
2. Aunt :
3. Nephew :
4. Niece :
5. Male Cousin :
6. Female Cousin :

Role Play :

1. Who is your father's brother?
2. Who is your father's father?
3. Who is your father's mother?
4. How are you related to your parents ?

Answer to Practice A:

1. Ich habe einen Bruder.
2. Du hast eine Schwester.
3. Er hat einen Großvater.
4. Sie hat eine Großmutter.
5. Es hat eine schöne Frage.

6. Wir haben einen Onkel.
7. Ihr habt eine Tante.
8. Sie haben eine Nichte.
9. Sie haben einen Neffe.

Answer to Practice B

1. der Onkel
2. die Tante
3. der Neffe
4. der Nichte
5. der Cousin
6. die Cousine

Scan the QR code to play the audio

Pronunciation Practice:

ich haben	I have
du hast	You have
Es hat	It has
wir haben	we have
ihr habt	you have
sie haben	they have
Ich habe einen Vater.	I have a Father:
Du hast eine Schwester	You(Informal) have a Sister

Er hat viele Brüder.	He has lot of Brothers
sie hat eine Tochter.	She has a Daughter
Es hat viele Fragen.	It has many questions
Wir haben einen Sohn.	We have a Son
Ihr habt eine Familie.	You all have a Family
sie haben eine Großmutter / Oma.	They have a Grandmother
Sie haben einen Großvater/ Opa.	You (Formal) have a Grandfather
Meine Familie	My Family
mutter	mother
vater	father
sohn	son
tochter	teacher
schwester	sister
bruder	brother
tante	aunt
onkel	uncle
cousine/cousin	cousin
nichte	niece

Telling Time

Die Uhrzeit - The Clock Timings

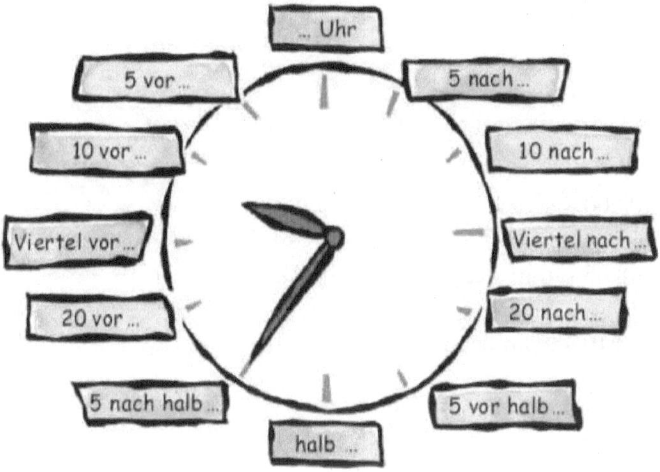

Objective- To discuss the German's formal and Informal Time and Adverbs of Time

Concept A: Informell Zeit

- vor: to
- Uhr: o'clock

- nach: past
- kurz: short of
- Viertel: quarter(15 minutes)
- am Morgen: am
- halb: half-an-hour(30 minutes)
- am Abend: pm

Example:

- 08:00 – acht Uhr
- 08:05 – fünf nach acht
- 08:10 – zehn nach acht
- 08:15 – Viertel nach acht
- 08:20 – zwanzig nach acht
- 08:25 – fünfundzwanzig nach acht / fünf vor halb neun
- 08:30 – halb neun
- 08:35 – fünf nach halb neun / fünfundzwanzig vor neun
- 08:02 - zwei nach acht
- 08:40 - zwanzig vor neun
- 08:45 – Viertel vor neun
- 08:50 – zehn vor neun

- 08: 55 – fünf vor neun

Concept B: Formell Zeit - 24 hour concept

- 20:00 – zwanzig Uhr
- 20:05 – zwanzig Uhr fünf Minuten
- 20:10 – zwanzig Uhr zehn Minuten
- 20:15 – zwanzig Uhr fünfzehn Minuten
- 20: 20 – zwanzig Uhr zwanzig Minuten
- 20:25 – zwanzig Uhr fünfundzwanzig Minuten
- 20:30 –zwanzig Uhr dreißig Minuten
- 20:35 – zwanzig Uhr fünfunddreißig Minuten
- 20:40 – zwanzig Uhr vierzig Minuten
- 20:45 – zwanzig Uhr fünfundvierzig Minuten
- 20:50 – zwanzig Uhr fünfzig Minuten
- 20:55 – zwanzig Uhr fünfundfünfzig Minuten

Concept C: Adverbs of Time

- Gestern — yesterday
- Vorgestern: Day before yesterday

- Heute — today
- Morgen — tomorrow
- Über Morgen - Day after Tomorrow
- Morgens — mornings
- Nachmittag — in the afternoon
- Nachts /Abends — evening, at night
- Täglich- Daily
- Bald - Soon
- Sofort - Immediately

Practice A: Formal Time

1. Past :
2. short of:
3. to :
4. quarter(15 minutes) :
5. half-an-hour(30 minutes) :

Practice B: Informal Time:

1. Hour:
2. 20:00:
3. 20:10:
4. 20:15:
5. 20:25:

Practice C: Adverbs of Time:

1. Yesterday:
2. Today:
3. Tomorrow:

Answer to Practice A:

1. Nach
2. Kurz
3. Vor
4. Viertel
5. Halb

Answer to Practice B:

1. Uhr
2. zwanzig Uhr
3. zwanzig Uhr zehn Minuten
4. zwanzig Uhr fünfzehn Minuten
5. zwanzig Uhr fünfundzwanzig Minuten

Answer to Practice C:

1. Yesterday - Gestern
2. Today - Heute
3. Tomorrow - Morgen

Scan the QR code to play the audio

Pronunciation Practice:

vor	to
Uhr	o' clock
nach	past
kurz	short of
nachViertel	quarter (15 minutes)
am Morgen	AM
halb	half-an-hour(30 minutes)
am Abend	PM

acht Uhr	8:00
fünf nach acht	8:05
zehn nach acht	8:10
Viertel nach acht	8:15
zwanzig nach acht	8:20
halb neun	8:30
zweinachacht	8:02
zwanzig vor neun	8:40
zehn vor neun	8:50
fünf vor neun	8:55
Formell Zeit	24 Hour
zwanzig Uhr	20:00
zwanzig Uhr fünf	20:05
zwanzig Uhr zehn	20:10
zwanzig Uhr fünfzehn	20:15
zwanzig Uhr zwanzig	20:20
zwanzig Uhr fünfundzwanzig	20:25
zwanzig Uhr dreißig	20:30
zwanzig Uhr fünfunddreißig	20:35
zwanzig Uhr vierzig	20:40

zwanzig Uhr fünfundvierzig	20:45
zwanzig Uhr fünfundfünfzig	20:55
acht uhr fuhnfundvierzig	8:45
Gestern	Yesterday
Vor Gestern	Day before yesterday
Heute	Today
Morgen	Tomorrow
Über Morgen	Day after Tomorrow
Morgens	Mornings
Nachmittag	In the afternoon
Nachts	Evening
Abends	at night
Täglich	Daily
Bald	Soon
Sofort	Immediately

Verb

A verb is a word, which shows action or position or being. The original form of a verb is called the "infinitive form". This infinitive form is conjugated according to the subject of the sentence and is called conjugated depending upon the number and person. In some languages, gender also plays a role in conjugation, but not in German.

In German, all the verbs, except a few, end with –en.

Objective - To discuss the German's Verb Conjugation of 'To be' and implement it in the Sentences.

Concept A : Conjugation of Verb 'to be' : (Sein)

- Sein - to be
- ich bin - I am
- du bist - you are
- er/sie/es ist - he/she/it is
- wir sind - we are
- ihr seid - you are

- Sie sind - they are

Concept B: Implementation of the verb in the Sentences :

- I am intelligent : Ich bin intelligent.
- You are a Student : Du bist ein Student.
- He is a Doctor : Er ist Arzt.
- She is a Teacher : Sie ist Lehrerin.
- It is a beautiful weather : Es ist ein schönes Wetter.
- We are friends : Wir sind Freunde.
- You all are colleagues : Ihr seid Kollegen.
- They are farmers : Sie sind Bauern.
- You are a German Teacher : Sie sind Deutsch Lehrer.

Practice A : Sein Conjugation (To be): Translate the following in German.

1. Ich (I) = am (....)
2. Du (you) (Informal) = are(....)
3. Er (He) = is(.....)
4. Es (It) = is(.....)
5. sie (She) = is(.....)

6. Wir(We) = are(.....)
7. Ihr(You all) = are(.....)
8. sie(They) = are(.....)
9. Sie(You) (Formal/Polite) = are(.....)

Practice B : Translate the following in German.

1. I am clever
2. You are naughty
3. She is beautiful
4. He is tall
5. It is great
6. We are not friends
7. You all are small
8. They are Ugly

Answers

Practice A:

1. Ich bin
2. Du bist
3. Er- ist

4. es - ist
5. sie - ist
6. Wir sind
7. Ihr seid
8. sie - sind
9. Sie - sind

Practice B:

1. Ich bin schlau.
2. Du bist ungezogen.
3. Sie ist schön.
4. Er ist groß.
5. Es ist toll.
6. Wir sind keine Freunde.
7. Ihr seid alle klein.
8. Sie sind hässlich.

Scan the QR code to play the audio

Pronunciation Practice:

Sein	to be
Ich bin intelligent.	I am intelligent
Du bist ein Student.	You are a Student
Er ist Arzt.	He is a Doctor
sie ist Lehrerin.	She is a Teacher
Es ist ein schönes Wetter.	It is a beautiful weather
Wir sind Freunde.	We are friends
Ihr seid Kollegen.	You all are colleagues
sie sind Bauern.	They are farmers
Sie sind Deutsch Lehrer.	You are a German Teacher

Nouns- Gender, Plural

Objective: I should be able to use the nouns in my speech and also identify the gender of the nouns and the plural forms

Concept A: What are nouns?

- Nouns in German are similar to nouns in English. But the nouns in German should always start with a capital letter. Example: Katze (cat), Mann (Man), Lehrerin (Female teacher) etc.
- Even if the nouns are in the middle of a sentence, they should be written with a capital letter in the beginning
- Nouns in German have a peculiar feature: They are addressed with articles like der, die, das, dem, den, des etc

Some nouns for practice:

- Das Jahr (pronounced as Yahr) : Year
- Das Beispiel : Example
- Das Haus : house
- Der Tag: Day
- Die Monate: Month
- Die Arbeit: Work
- Das Hand: hand

Concept B: Gender of the nouns

The Nouns in German language as explained in concept A is addressed with the articles.

These articles indicate the gender of the nouns.

- Der : Shows that the noun is Masculine gender
- Die : Shows that the noun is Feminine gender
- Das : shows that the noun is Neuter gender

Example:

- Der Tag indicates that Tag is masculine gender
- Die Arbeit indicates that Arbeit is feminine gender
- Das Beispiel indicates that it is neuter gender

Concept C:

- Plural indicates the counting of objects more than one. It is indicated by the article "Die"
- In German, we have singular and plural
- Singular is used for indicating any singular object

Example: Der Tisch (Table) here is masculine gender and is singular

The plural of Tisch is die Tische (Tables). Here the plural is indicated by the article "die"

In plural, the nouns undergo some changes. See the below image:

Suffix

Plural form

- -nis, -ling, ig, -ich
  -e plural
- -tum
  -er + umlaut plural
- -chen, -lein
  -no change
- -er*, -el*, -en
  -no change
- -e
  -(e)n plural

NOTE:feminine nouns ending with -er, or -el take the -(e)n plural

The plural forms change as per the words given. Hence, in order to understand their forms, you have to learn and practise more nouns.

We have 4 cases in German : Nominativ, Akkusativ, Dative and Genitive. The articles for each of these cases are different for singular and plural. The articles which we learnt in this session are for the Nominative case, the most basic case.

Practice A: Identify the nouns from the below:

arbeiten, Arbeit, Körper, machen, putzen, Haus, Hand, Stuhl, wohnen

Practice B: Identify the masculine, feminine and neuter gender:

Der Tisch, Die Frau, Der Mann, Das Kind, Der Monat, Das Auto, Die Welt, der Mensch, die Stadt

Practice C: Write the plural form of the above words given in Practice B.

Check out the video given below and make a note of all the nouns :

Write a small text on the nouns you have learnt from the above video and also the nouns which you have learnt in this session.

Scan the QR code to play the video for understanding plural of nouns in German and make note of them:

Answers to Practice A:

1. Arbeit
2. Körper
3. Haus
4. Hand
5. Stuhl

Answers to Practice B:

1. Der Tisch: Masculine

2. Die Frau: Feminine
3. Der Mann: Masculine
4. Das Kind: Neuter
5. Der Monat: Masculine
6. Das Auto: Neuter
7. Die Welt: Feminine
8. Der Mensch: Masculine
9. Die Stadt: Feminine

Answers to Practice C:

1. Die Tische
2. Die Frauen
3. Die Männer
4. Die Kinder
5. Die Monate
6. Die Autos
7. Die Welten
8. Die Menschen
9. Die Städte

Scan the QR code to play the audio

🔊 Pronunciation Practice:

Katze	Cat
Mann	Man
Lehrerin	Female teacher
Das Jahr (pronounced as Yahr)	Year
Das Beispiel	Example
Das Haus	House

Der Tag	Day
Die Monate	Month
Die Arbeit	Work
Das Hand	Hand
Der	Masculine gender noun
Die	Feminine gender noun
Das	Neuter gender noun
Der Tisch	Table(singular)
die Tische	Tables (plural)

Nominativ, Akkusativ and Dativ

Objective : To understand the usage of different cases in German language

Concept A: Nominativ

This case is used for writing the subject in a sentence.

The articles for Nominativ is given below:

Masculine	**Feminine**	**Neuter**	**plural**
Der	Die	Das	Die

Example:

1. M : Der Mann ist klug (The man is clever)
2. F : Die Frau ist nett (The lady is nice)
3. N: Das Kind ist intelligent (The child is intelligent)

Concept B: Akkusativ

1. This case is used for objects. An Object can be anything, a person or a thing.
2. This case is also used for showing movement
3. This case comes when certain prepositions or verbs are used

The articles for Akkusativ are given below:

Masculine	**Feminine**	**Neuter**	**Plural**
Den	Die	Das	Die

Example:

1. M: Ich habe den Mann gesehen.
2. F : Ich suche die Frau
3. N: Ich finde das Kind schön.

Concept C: Dativ

1. This is used for indirect Object
2. This is also used for stationary objects (objects with no movement)
3. Dative case comes when certain prepositions or verbs come

Dativ is also used with prepositions like :

Preposition	Pronunciation	Meaning
aus	ows	from, out of
außer	OW-sir	except for, besides
bei	bye	at, near
mit	mit	with, by
nach	nahk	after, to
seit	zite	since, for
von	fawn	from, by
zu	tsoo	to, at

Masculine **Feminine** **Neuter** **Plural**

Dem Der dem den + n (extra n in noun)

Examples:

1. Ich schreibe dem Mann(der Mann) einen Brief. : I write a letter to the man
2. Ich gebe der Frau die Hut (die Frau): I give the lady the hat.
3. Sie kommen aus dem Museum (Das Museum) : They are coming out from the Museum
4. Ich arbeite mit meinen Händen (Die Hände) : I work with my hands

Here, the plural is Hände, but because we have dativ plural, we add an extra 'n' in the noun.

Note: All the above cases have almost the same endings for possessive pronomen.

Example:meinen Tisch, seinem Auto etc

1. Das ist mein Tisch.
2. Ich male meinen Tisch.
3. Das Buch liegt auf meinem Tisch.

We also have personal pronouns for different cases and also different endings for adjectives used according to the cases.

PRACTICE A:

Please give 5 sentences using the Akkusativ, Nominativ and Dativ

PRACTICE B: Translate to German:

1. I come from England.
2. I write a letter to my wife.
3. I work with my hands.
4. The child is clever and intelligent.
5. The man gives the hat to the child

PRACTICE C: Fill in the blanks with definite articles.

1. Er arbeitet mit ___ Händen.
2. Ich schicke ___ Frau einen Brief
3. Es kommt mit ___ Bus
4. Du gehst mit ___ Mann zur Arbeit.
5. Die Mutter kauft ___ Tochter das Kleid.

Practice D. Make sentences in Nominativ, Akkusativ, Dativ accordingly using the below words:

1. Der Weihnachtsmann (Santaclaus)

2. Das Kind (Child)
3. Das Geschenk (Gift)
4. geben (to give)
5. ein (one)
6. Die Frau (Lady)
7. Der Mann (Man)
8. Die Kinder (Children)

Practice E: Match the pairs:

A	B
1. Ich gebe	a. zur Arbeit
2. Ich gehe	b. mit dem Computer
3. Sie arbeitet	c. dir ein Glas Wasser

Watch the video for more information on Dativ:

ANSWERS TO PRACTICE A:

1. Ich wohne in einem kleinen Haus: Dativ
2. Das ist ein Tisch: Nominativ
3. Ich kaufe eine Tasche: Akkusativ
4. Die Mutter schicke ihrer Tochter eine E-Mail: Akkusativ and Dativ
5. Er ist sehr nett: Nominativ

ANSWERS TO PRACTICE B:

1. I come from England: Ich komme aus England.

2. I write letter to my wife : Ich schreibe meiner Frau einen Brief.
3. I work with my hands : Ich arbeite mit meinen Händen.
4. The child is clever and intelligent: Das Kind ist klug und intelligent
5. The man gives the hat to the child : Der Mann gibt dem Kind den Hut.

ANSWERS TO PRACTICE C:

1. Er arbeitet mit den Händen.
2. Ich schicke der Frau einen Brief.
3. Es kommt mit dem Bus.
4. Du gehst mit dem Mann zur Arbeit.
5. Die Mutter kauft der Tochter das Kleid.

ANSWERS TO PRACTICE D:

1. Der Weihnachtsmann kommt mit den Geschenken.
2. Das Kind wartet auf den Weihnachtsmann.
3. Das Geschenk ist mit dem Kind.
4. Ich gebe dir ein Buch.
5. Die Frau ist nett.
6. Der Mann hat eine Tochter.

7. Die Kinder spielen Fußball.

8. Ein Sänger ist eine Person, der singt.

ANSWERS TO PRACTICE E:

1. c

2. b

3. a

Scan the QR code to play the audio

Pronunciation Practice:

Der	Masculine
Die	Feminine
Das	Neuter
Die	plural
Der Mann ist klug	The man is clever
Die Frau ist nett	The lady is nice
Das Kind is intelligent	The child is intelligent
Den	Masculine
aus	from, out of
außer	except for, besides
bei	at, near
mit	with, by
nach	after, to
seit	since, for
von	from, by
zu	to, at
Ich schreibe einen Brief dem Mann(der Mann)	I write letter to the man

Ich gebe der Frau die Hut (die Frau)	I give the lady a hat
Sie kommen aus dem Museum (Das Museum)	They come out from the Museum
Ich arbeite mit meinen Händen (Die Hände)	I work with my hands

Expression of Time, Manner and Place

Objective: To understand how to use expressions of time, place and manner in German language

CONCEPT A : How do we place the Time adverb in a sentence.

When several adverbs are used in the same sentence in German, the sentence becomes more complex, and they must appear in this strict order:

German sentences will often seem a bit different from how we would say things in English. In English, for example, we tend to put the place before the time, but in German the time always goes before the place.

Look at the following English sentences:

- I go to school by bus at 08:00.
- I play with my dog in the park every day.

Now look at the difference in word order when the sentences are translated to German. You can see how they follow the time, manner, place (TMP) rule.

- Ich fahre am 8 Uhr mit dem Bus zur Schule.
- Ich spiele täglich mit meinem Hund im Park.

If there are two adverbial phrases from the same group in a sentence, they follow the same order as in English, eg:

1. zweimal – twice
2. die Woche – week

so:

1. zweimal die Woche - twice a week
2. jeden Tag um acht Uhr – every day at 08:00

The verb (main or auxiliary) is still the second idea.

Past participles and infinitives go to the end.

- Wir werden am Dienstag (1) schnell (2) in die Stadt (3) gehen. - We'll quickly go into town on Tuesday.
- Sie kann immer (1) sehr gut (2) singen. - She can always sing well. (No adverb of place in this sentence).

- Ich lese jeden Tag (1) eine halbe Stunde (2) im Bett. (3) - I read in bed for half an hour every day. (No adverb of manner).

CONCEPT B: Sentence Structure in German:

1. Simple, declarative sentences are identical in German and English: Subject, verb, other.
2. The verb is always the second element in a German sentence.
3. With compound verbs, the second part of the verb goes last, but the conjugated part is still second.
4. German sentences are usually "time, manner, place."
5. After a subordinate clause / conjunction, the verb goes last.

Summary: In a normal sentence, the verb should always be in 2nd position and the sentence order should be in TIME, MANNER, PLACE (TMP) order.

Verb position changes with the connectors/conjunctions.

PRACTICE A: Can you identify the time, manner and place phrases in these sentences?

1. Wir sehen abends nicht gern Horrorfilme.

2. Ich war meistens samstags mit Freunden im Einkaufszentrum.
3. Du kannst morgen hoffentlich bei mir übernachten.
4. Sie sind letztes Jahr mit uns nach Irland gefahren.

PRACTICE B: Place the TMP adverbs in the right place in the sentence.

1. Ich frühstücke draußen. (mit meiner Familie; manchmal)
2. Sie wird als Sprachassistentin arbeiten. (in Graz; nächstes Jahr)
3. Wir spielen Doppelkopf. (einmal im Monat; mit Freunden; normalerweise)
4. Er kann nicht kommen. (zur Arbeit; heute; leider)

PRACTICE C: Write 5 sentences in German following the TMP rule

Watch the below video for TMP:

ANSWERS TO PRACTICE A:

- Wir sehen abends nicht gern Horrorfilme. - We don't like watching horror films in the evening. (Literally: We don't watch horror films gladly).

Time **Manner**
Place

abends nicht
gern no place

- Ich war meistens samstags mit Freunden im Einkaufszentrum. - I was usually in the shopping centre with my friends on Saturdays.

Time **Manner** **Place**

meistens/samstags mit Freunden im Einkaufszentrum

- Du kannst morgen hoffentlich bei mir übernachten. - You can sleep round at my house tomorrow, hopefully.

Time **Manner** **Place**

morgen hoffentlich bei mir

- Sie sind letztes Jahr mit uns nach Irland gefahren. - They went to Ireland with us last year.

Time **Manner** **Place**

letztes Jahr mit uns nach Irland

ANSWERS TO PRACTICE B:

- Ich frühstücke manchmal mit meiner Familie draußen. - I sometimes have breakfast outside with my family.

Time **Manner** **Place**

manchmal mit meiner Familie draußen

- Sie wird nächstes Jahr als Sprachassistentin in Graz arbeiten. - She will work as a foreign language assistant in Graz next year.

Time **Manner** **Place**

nächstes Jahr als Sprachassistentin in Graz

- Wir spielen normalerweise einmal im Monat mit Freunden Doppelkopf. - We usually play Doppelkopf once a month with friends.

Time **Manner** **Place**

normalerweise mit Freunden none

- Er kann heute leider nicht zur Arbeit kommen. - Unfortunately, he can't come to work today.

Time **Manner** **Place**

heute
leider zur Arbeit

Scan the QR code to play the audio

🔊 Pronunciation Practice:

zweimal	twice
die Woche	week
zweimal die Woche	twice a week
Jeden Tag um acht Uhr	every day at 08:00
Wir werden am Dienstag schnell in die Stadt gehen.	We'll quickly go into town on Tuesday.
Sie kann immer sehr gut singen.	She can always sing well.
Ich lese jeden Tag eine halbe Stunde im Bett	I read in bed for half an hour every day.
Ich frühstücke manchmal mit meiner Familie draußen.	I sometimes have breakfast outside with my family.
Sie wird nächstes Jahr als Sprachassistentin in Graz arbeiten.	She will work as a foreign language assistant in Graz next year.
Wir spielen normalerweise einmal im Monat mit Freunden Doppelkopf.	We usually play Doppelkopf once a month with friends.
Er kann heute leider nicht zur Arbeit kommen.	Unfortunately, he can't come to work today.

Review 2

Objective: To revise the concept of whatever done so far

Concept A:"sein" and "haben" revision

Sein: to be

Singular

ich **bin**	I am
du bist/ Sie(formal) **sind**	you are/ you(formal) are
er/sie/es **ist**	he/she/it is

Plural:

wir **sind**	we are
ihr **seid**	you are(as in: you guys are)
sie **sind**	they are

<u>Haben: to have</u>

Singular

ich **habe**	I have
du **hast**/ Sie **haben**	you have/ you(formal) have
er/sie/es **hat**	he/she/it has

Plural

wir **haben**	we have
ihr **habt**	you have (as in: you guys have)
sie **haben**	they have

Concept B: Time in German

Die Zeit: Time

Die Uhr: Clock

You can use the following phrases as a guide when talking about time and dates in German:

- **Wissen Sie, wie viel Uhr es ist?**(Do you know what time it is?)
- **Wie viel Uhr ist es?**(What time is it?)
- **Haben Sie ein paar Minuten Zeit?**(Do you have a couple of minutes to spare?)
- **Um wie viel Uhr fahren Sie ab?**(What time do you leave?)

- **Es ist früh.**(It's early.)
- **Du kommst aber spät.**(You're really late.)
- **Welchen Tag haben wir heute?**(What day is today?)
- **Heute ist Freitag.**(Today is Friday.)
- **Der Wievielte ist heute?**(What's today's date?)
- **Heute ist der dritte Mai.**(Today is the third of May.)
- **Alarm:**Der Alarm
- **Alarm Ruf**: Alarm call

Vocabulary for telling time in German:

- **Uhr**– The German equivalent of o'clock, used to denominate full hours.
- **Um**– Means as in "Let's meet at four o'clock".
- **Vor**– Before like in "Seven minutes before midnight".
- **Nach**– The antonym of vor, of course meaning after.
- **Viertel**– This means quarter like in quarter past/quarter to.
- **Halb**– meaning half and is used to denote the half hour intervals between full hours. More on this below.

Concept C: Telling family members in German

Revise all the family members in German language:

- mother die Mutter
- sister lie Schwester
- cousin die Cousine
- father der Vater
- brother der Bruder
- cousin der Cousin
- son der Sohn
- aunt die Tante
- niece die Nichte
- daughter die Tochter
- uncle der Onkel
- nephew der neffe

Concept D: Nouns, gender, plural

Write the gender with articles and plural of the below nouns:

Mutter, Katze, Männer, Kind, Mädchen, Frau, Höflichkeit, Eidechse

Concept E: Nominativ, Akkusativ and Dativ

	Masculine	**Feminine**	**Neuter**	**Plural**
Nominativ	der	die	das	die
Akkusativ	den	die	das	die
Dativ	dem	der	dem	den
Genitive	des	der	des	der

Concept F: Expressions of Time, Manner and Place:

Time

- Jeden Sonntag
- Jeden Samstag
- Während der Woche
- Um 7 Uhr

Manner

- Mit meiner Familie
- Mit meinen Freunden
- Mit dem Bus
- Mit der Straßenbahn

Place

- Nach Deutschland
- Nach Österreich
- Nach Schule
- Nach Hause

Findet

- Hallo! Ich heiße Uter und
- ich fahre oft nach Deutschland.
- Ich fahre jeden Sonntag mit
- meiner Familie nach Österreich.
- Ich stehe jeden Samstag
- um 6 Uhr auf. Ich gehe sehr
- gern mit meinen Freunden zu
- Fuß in die Stadt. Ich fahre während
- der Woche mit dem Bus zur Schule.
- Otto, der Busfahrer, kommt um
- 7 Uhr pünktlich. Ich liebe die
- Busfahrt! Ich fahre nach der Schule

- mit der Straßenbahn nach Hause.

Practice A:

Make a family tree of your family

Practice B: Please tell the below in German language:

1. 12: 30
2. 13:40
3. 4:15
4. 9:00

Practice C: Give 5 sentences using Time, Manner, Place.

Write a paragraph on the below topics using nouns with correct articles, TMP, sein/haben, correct usage of Nominativ, Akkusativ, Dativ

1. Meine Familie
2. Ihre Hobbys
3. Mein Beruf

Answers to Practice A: Der Familienstammbaum (Family tree)

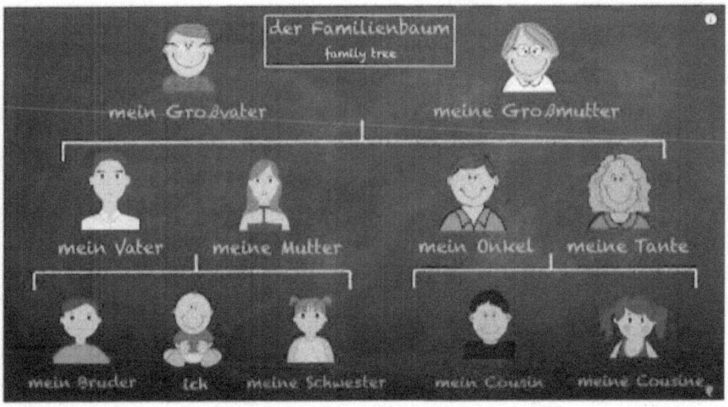

Answers to Practice B:

1. 12:30: halb eins
2. 13:40: dreizehn Uhr vierzig Minuten
3. 4:15: viertel nach vier
4. 9:00: neun Uhr

Answers to Practice C:

1. Ich war meistens samstags mit Freunden im Einkaufszentrum.
2. Wir werden am Dienstag schnell in die Stadt gehen
3. Sie kann immer sehr gut singen.
4. Ich kann am Montag zur Arbeit gehen.
5. Sie sind letztes Jahr mit uns nach Irland gefahren.

Practice Test 1

Objective: To check if the concepts done so far are understood or not

Q1 : Introduce yourself in German using the below points:

1. Your name
2. Your education/profession
3. Your residence
4. Your mobile number/telephone number
5. Your hobbies

Q2: Translate the below sentences to German:

1. I have a book
2. That is a table
3. She writes a letter to her friend
4. I search for the pen
5. He types the letter with the computer

Q3: Write down the articles of Nominativ, Akkusativ and Dativ in all the 3 genders

Q4: Write the plural forms of the below:

Example:der Satz - die Sätze, die Woche - die Wochen

1. die Minute - die, die Sekund - die
2. die Frage - die, die Antwort - die
3. das Kind - die, der Mensch - die
4. das Auto - die, die Straße - die
5. das Jahr - die, die Stunde - die
6. der Junge - die, das Mädchen -die
7. der Mann - die, die Frau - die
8. das Buch - die, die Zeitung - die
9. der Tag - die, der Monat - die
10. das Geschäft - die, die Schule - die
11. der Schuh - die, die Hand - die
12. das Zimmer - die, das Bett - die
13. der Freund - die, die Freundin - die

Q5: Write the conjugations of sein and haben

Q6: Translate the below passage to English:

Zu meiner Familie gehören vier Personen. Die Mutter bin ich und dann gehört natürlich mein Mann dazu. Wir haben zwei Kinder, einen Sohn, der sechs Jahre alt ist und eine dreijährige Tochter.

Wir wohnen in einem kleinen Haus mit einem Garten. Dort können die Kinder ein bisschen spielen. Unser Sohn kommt bald in die Schule, unsere Tochter geht noch eine Zeit lang in den Kindergarten. Meine Kinder sind am Nachmittag zu Hause. So arbeite ich nur halbtags.

Eigentlich gehören zu unserer Familie auch noch die Großeltern. Sie wohnen nicht bei uns. Sie haben ein Haus in der Nähe. Die Kinder gehen sie oft besuchen.

Answer to Q1:

1. Mein Name ist Aruna.
2. Ich bin Lehrerin von Beruf. Ich habe meine Ausbildung zum Sanskrit und Deutsch gemacht.
3. Ich wohne in Bengaluru, Shankar Straße.
4. Meine Handynummer ist --------------.
5. Meine Hobbys sind reisen, einkaufen, neue Sprache lernen, tanzen und Bücher lesen.

Answer to Q2:

1. Ich habe ein Buch.
2. Das ist ein Tisch

3. Sie schreibt ihrem Freund einen Brief.
4. Ich suche ein Kuli/Kugelschreiber
5. Er tippt mit dem Computer den Brief.

Answer to Q3:

Nominative: Plural: die

M F N

Der die das

Akkusativ: Plural: die

M F N

Den die das

Dativ: Plural: den + n (extra n in the noun in plural)

M F N

Dem der dem

Answer to Q4

1. die Minute - die Minuten, die Sekunde - die Sekunden
2. die Frage - die Fragen, die Antwort - die Antworten

3. das Kind - die Kinder, der Mensch - die Menschen
4. das Auto - die Autos, die Straße - die Straßen
5. das Jahr - die Jahre, die Stunde - die Stunden
6. der Junge - die Jungen, das Mädchen - die Mädchen
7. der Mann - die Männer, die Frau - die Frauen
8. das Buch - die Bücher, die Zeitung - die Zeitungen
9. der Tag - die Tage, der Monat - die Monate
10. das Geschäft - die Geschäfte, die Schule - die Schulen
11. der Schuh - die Schuhe, die Hand - die Hände
12. das Zimmer - die Zimmer, das Bett - die Betten
13. der Freund - die Freunde, die Freundin - die Freundinnen

Answer to Q5:

Sein:

Ich bin wir sind

Du bist

Sie sind ihr seid

Er ist

Sie ist

Es ist sie sind

Haben:

Ich habe wir haben

Du hast

Sie haben ihr hat

Er hat

Es hat

Sie hat sie haben

Answer to Q6:

My family consists of 4 people. I am the mother and of course my husband is one of them. We have 2 children, a son, who is 6 years old and a 3-year-old daughter.

We live in a small house with a small garden. There the children can play a little. Our son comes soon to the school, our daughter goes a little late to the Kindergarten.

My children are at home by afternoon. Hence, I work only for half-days

Actually the grandparents also belong to our family. They don't live with us. They have a house in the neighbourhood. The children often go to visit them.

Possessiv Pronomen

Objective: To understand what possessive pronouns are and use them in our language.

Concept A: Possessive pronouns, like English language, are used for the same purpose.

In German language, we call them 'Possessiv Pronomen'

Possessive pronouns indicate possession. There are dependent and independent possessive pronouns in German grammar, both types must agree with their noun in case, gender and number.

Concept B: How are possessiv Pronomen used?

Dependent possessive pronouns come before nouns, which is why they are also called possessive articles. The chart below provides an overview of the singular and plural forms of dependent possessive pronouns in Nominativ, Akkusativ, Dative and Genitive cases.

We have learnt about pronouns like ich, du, sie, er etc.

The same pronouns will be converted to possessive pronouns and when used along with the cases, gender and number, we can start using the Possessiv Pronomen.

Concept C: Below is the list of Possessiv Pronomen:

		ich	du	er	sie	es	wir	ihr	sie
nominative	m/n	mein	dein	sein	ihr	sein	unser	euer	ihr
	f/pl	meine	deine	seine	ihre	seine	unsere	eure	ihre
accusative	m	meinen	deinen	seinen	ihren	seinen	unseren	euren	ihren
	n	mein	dein	sein	ihr	sein	unser	euer	ihr
	f/pl	meine	deine	seine	ihre	seine	unsere	eure	ihre
dative	m/n	meinem	deinem	seinem	ihrem	seinem	unserem	eurem	ihrem
	f	meiner	deiner	seiner	ihrer	seiner	unserer	eurer	ihrer
	pl	meinen	deinen	seinen	ihren	seinen	unseren	euren	ihren
genitive	m/n	meines	deines	seines	ihres	seines	unseres	eures	ihres
	f/pl	meiner	deiner	seiner	ihrer	seiner	unserer	eurer	ihrer

Concept D: Let us see some examples:

1. Das ist mein Koffer (That is my suitcase)
2. Es bedarf deiner Hilfe, nicht meiner. (It needs your help, not mine)
3. Ihr Auto ist sehr gut (Her car is very good)
4. Wir kommen mit unserem Auto (We come in our car)
5. Brauchst du seiner Hilfe? (Do you need his help)

Practice A: Fill in the blanks

1. (sie) Rücken tut weh.
2. Er hat (er) Brille vergessen.
3. Ich finde (ihr) Vorschlag gut.
4. Wir sind zu (wir) Großeltern gefahren.
5. Hast du von (ich) Kuchen gekostet?

Practice B: Choose the correct dependent or independent possessive pronoun:

1. Ich habe ___ Freundin gerade eine SMS geschrieben. Hast du ___ heute auch schon eine SMS geschrieben?
2. Die kleine Lisa hat ____ Lieblingsspielzeug in den Kindergarten mitgenommen. Der kleine Otto hat ____ zu Hause vergessen.
3. ____ Lehrer ist viel besser als _____.
4. Sie füttern gerade ----------- Hund. ___ haben wir vorhin schon Fressen gegeben.
5. Entlang ____ Hauses wachsen Sonnenblumen. Was wächst um ____ Haus herum?

Write a conversation using Possessive Pronomen

Answers to Practice A:

1. Ihr Rücken tut weh.
2. Er hat seine Brille vergessen.
3. Ich finde euren Vorschlag gut.
4. Wir sind zu unseren Großeltern gefahren.
5. Hast du von meinem Kuchen gekostet?

Answers to Practice B:

1. Ich habe meiner Freundin gerade eine SMS geschrieben. Hast du deiner heute auch schon eine SMS geschrieben?
2. Die kleine Lisa hat ihr Lieblingsspielzeug in den Kindergarten mitgenommen. Der kleine Otto hat sein zu Hause vergessen.
3. Mein Lehrer ist viel besser als eurer.
4. Sie füttern gerade ihren Hund. Unserem haben wir vorhin schon Fressen gegeben.
5. Entlang seines Hauses wachsen Sonnenblumen. Was wächst um euer Haus herum?

Scan the QR code to play the audio

🔊 **Pronunciation Practice:**

ich	I
du	you(informal)
er	he
sie	you(formal)
es	it
wir	we
ihr	you all(informal)
Das ist mein Koffer	That is my suitcase
Es bedarf deiner Hilfe, nicht meiner.	It needs your help, not mine

Ihr Auto ist sehr gut	Her car is very good
Wir kommen mit unserem Auto	We come in our car
Brauchst du seiner Hilfe?	Do you need his help?

Verb Conjugation-Regular and Personal Pronoun

Objective: To be able to conjugate regular verbs.

Concept A: Regular Verb Conjugation

Ich	-e
du	-st
er/sie/es	-t
Wir	-en-n
Ihr	-t
sie/Sie	-en -n

Concept B: Regular Verb Conjugation with examples

	Endings	**Example gehen**	**Example machen**
Ich	-e	Geh**e**	Mach**e**
Du	-st	Geh**st**	Mach**st**
Er, sie, es	-t	Geh**t**	Mach**t**
Wir	-en	Geh**en**	Mach**en**
Ihr	-t	Geh**t**	Mach**t**
sie, Sie	-en	Geh**en**	mach**en**

Concept C: Personal Pronouns

Person		**English**		**German**
Singular	1st	I	→	ich
	2nd	you (informal)	→	du
		You (formal)	→	Sie
	3rd	he	→	er
		she	→	sie
		it	→	es
Plural	1st	we	→	wir
	2nd	you all (informal)	→	ihr
		You all (formal)	→	Sie
	3rd	they	→	sie

PERSONAL PRONOUNS		
NOMINATIV	**AKKUSATIV**	**DATIV**
Ich	mich	mir
Du	Dich	dir
Er	Ihn	ihm
sie	Sir	ihr
Es	Es	ihm
Wir	Uns	uns
Ihr	Euch	euch
sie	sie	ihnen
Sie	Sie	Ihnen

Practice A: Write the conjugation of the following regular verbs

- lachen
- spielen
- denken
- sagen
- suchen
- wohnen

Answers Practice A:

English	German infinitive	ich	du	er/sie/es	wir	ihr	Sie/sie (pl.)
to laugh	*lachen*	*lache*	*lachst*	*lacht*	*lachen*	*lacht*	*lachen*
to live	*leben*	*lebe*	*lebst*	*lebt*	*leben*	*lebt*	*leben*
to live/reside	*wohnen*	*wohne*	*wohnst*	*wohnt*	*wohnen*	*wohnt*	*wohnen*
to love	*lieben*	*liebe*	*liebst*	*liebt*	*lieben*	*liebt*	*lieben*
to need	*brauchen*	*brauche*	*brauchst*	*braucht*	*brauchen*	*braucht*	*brauchen*
to play	*spielen*	*spiele*	*spielst*	*spielt*	*spielen*	*spielt*	*spielen*
to say	*sagen*	*sage*	*sagst*	*sagt*	*sagen*	*sagt*	*sagen*
to seek	*suchen*	*suche*	*suchst*	*sucht*	*suchen*	*sucht*	*suchen*
to think	*denken*	*denke*	*denkst*	*denkt*	*denken*	*denkt*	*denken*
to visit	*besuchen*	*besuche*	*besuchst*	*besucht*	*besuchen*	*besucht*	*besuchen*

Scan the QR code to play the audio

Pronunciation Practice:

gehst	go
geht	goes
gehen	go
mache	make
machst	do
macht	power
machen	do
mich	me
dich	you
ihn	him
sie	she
es	it
uns	us
euch	to you
mir	me
dir	to you
ihm	him

Hobbies

Objective: To understand and learn the different hobbies in German language.

Concept A: Das Hobby, die Hobbys

How will you speak a few sentences about your hobbies?

Questions related to hobbies:

1. Was machen Sie/machst du am liebsten? (What do you do gladly/happily?)
2. Was sind Ihre/deine Hobbys? (What are your hobbies?)
3. Was machen Sie/machst du in Ihrer/deiner Freizeit? (What do you do in your freetime?)

Answers related to Hobbies

1. Mein Lieblings hobby/Lieblings hobbys ist/sind… (My favourite hobby/hobbies is/are...)

2. Ich …(list of hobbies in conjugated form according to subject

Example: Ich koche, reise, lese gern (I cook, travel, read gladly)

3. In meiner Freizeit...ich gern (In my freetime, I ----- gladly)

Example: In meiner Freizeit lese ich gern (In my freetime, I read gladly)

Concept B: Some hobbies for reference:

- lesen - reading
- Musik hören – listen to music
- Münzen/Briefmarken sammeln – to collect coins and stamps
- fotografieren – photography
- Rad fahren – bicycling
- joggen – jogging
- malen – painting
- tanzen – dancing
- singen – singing

- Briefmarken sammeln – collecting stamps
- ein Musikinstrument spielen – to play a musical instrument
- Zeichnen – drawing/sketching
- Kalligrafie – Calligraphy
- Internet surfen – surfing the internet
- Yoga machen – to do Yoga
- Aerobic machen – to do aerobics
- mit Freunde ausgehen – to go out with friends
- im Garten arbeiten – gardening
- Schwimmen – swimming
- Skifahren – skiing
- Schlittschuh laufen – ice skating
- Angeln – fishing
- Stricken – knitting
- Zeichnen – draw
- Wandern – hiking
- Kegeln – bowling
- Sport treiben – to do sports
- kochen – cooking

- backen – baking
- Fernsehen – watching tv
- laufen – walking
- Urlaub machen - holiday

Practice A: Write your hobbies list in German language

Practice B: Translate the below passage on hobbies:

Ich habe keine speziellen Hobbys. Ich denke, ich mache einfach gerne was alle jungen Leute so mögen. Ich mag es ins Kino zu gehen, im Park rumhängen, manchmal Karten spielen und viel über Musik und Leute und so quatschen. Wenn ich allein bin, spiele ich Computerspiele, sehe ich fern oder lade ich meine eigenen Videos auf YouTube hoch. Ich schätze mal, dass ich mich mit dem Computer ganz gut auskenne.

Answers to Practice A:

- Normalerweise lese gern Bücher. Manchmals koche ich auch.
- Außerdem kann ich auch gut malen, tanzen und singen.
- Ich lerne auch viele Sprachen in meiner Freizeit.

Answers to Practice B:

I don't have any special hobbies. I think I just like doing what all young people like. I like going to the movies, hanging out in the park, playing cards sometimes and chatting a lot about music, people and so on. When I am on my own I play computer games, watch TV, or upload my own YouTube videos. I guess my computer skills are not so bad.

Scan the QR code to play the audio

Pronunciation Practice:

Das Hobby	Hobby
Die Hobbys	Hobbies
Was machen Sie/machst du am liebsten?	What do you / do you like to do most?

Was sind Ihre/deine Hobbys?	What are your / your hobbies?
Was machen Sie/machst du in Ihrer/deiner Freizeit?	What do you / do you do in your / your free time?
Mein Lieblingshobby/Lieblingshobbys ist/sind…….	My favourite hobby/hobbies is/are…..
Ich …..	list of hobbies in conjugated form according to subject
Ich koche, reise, lese gern	I cook, travel, read gladly
In meiner Freizeit…….ich gern	In my freetime, I ----- gladly
In meiner Freizeit lese ich gern	In my freetime, I read gladly
lesen	reading
Musik hören	listen to music
Münzen sammeln	to collect coins and stamps
fotografieren	photography
radfahren	bicycling
joggen	jogging

malen	painting
singen	singing
tanzen	dancing
Briefmarken sammeln	collecting stamps
ein Musikinstrument spielen	to play a musical instrument
zeichnen	drawing/sketching
Kalligrafie	Calligraphy
Internet surfen	surfing the internet
Yoga machen	to do Yoga
Aerobic machen	to do aerobics
mit Freunde ausgehen	to go out with friends
im Garten arbeiten	gardening
Schwimmen	swimming
Skifahren	skiing
Schlittschuh laufen	ice skating
Angeln	fishing
Sport treiben	to do sports
Stricken	knitting
kochen	cooking

Kegeln	bowling
Wandern	hiking
backen	baking
Fernsehen	watching tv
laufen	walking
Urlaub machen	holiday

Irregular and Separable Verb Conjugation

Objective: To be able to conjugate irregular and separable verbs

Concept A: Irregular Verb conjugation

Irregular or strong verbs do not follow this pattern. They change in the du and er, sie, es forms as

Follows:

Fahren	sehen	lesen	essen	heißen
ich fahre	sehe	lese	esse	heiße
du fährst	siehst	liest	isst	heißt
er fährt	sieht	liest	isst	heißt
wir fahren	sehen	lesen	essen	heißen
ihr fahrt	seht	lest	esst	heißt
sie fahren	sehen	lesen	essen	heißen

Also

ich bin	habe
du bist	hast
er ist	hat
wir sind	haben
ihr seid	habt
sie sind	haben

Possible changes are:

- long e → ie (sehen)
- short e →i (essen)
- a → ä (fahren)
- au → äu (saufen)
- o→ ö (stoßen)

Concept B: Separable verbs' conjugation (Trennbare Verb)

Trennbare Verben

AUF STEHEN

EIN KAUFEN

AN ZIEHEN

LOS	GEHEN
AUF	RÄUMEN
AB	FAHREN
AN	FANGEN
FERN	SEHEN
ZURÜCK	KOMMEN

Concept C: Difference between main verb and separable verb

1. fahren – to travel ---- abfahren – to depart
2. stehen – to stand ----- aufstehen – to get up
3. kaufen – to buy --- einkaufen – to shop

Most prepositions can be made into separable prefer and most separable prefixes are originally prepositions. These prefixes change the new verb's meaning in a way that's often related to the origin of the meaning of the preposition. Here are some examples for the most common separable prefixes:

PREPOSMON / PREFIX **(general meaning)**	**EXAMPLE**	**ENGLISH**
AB- AWAY	ALFAHREN	deport

	ASAGEN	cancel
AN- TOWARDS	ANKOMMEN ANFANGEN	arrive begin
AUF – UP, ON	AUFSTEHEN AUFHÖREN	wake up stop
AUS – OUT, ALSO SUGGESTS COMPLETION	AUSSTEIGNEN AUSSTEHEN	get out of a traini stand somebody
EIN - IN	EINSTEIGNEN EINLADEN	get in (train) Invite
LOS – INDICATES BEGINNING SOMETHING	LOSGEHEN LOSBRECHEN	get started break loose/escape
MIT – WITH, DOING	MITBRINGEN MITLOMMEN	bring along come with
NACH – AFTER, FOLLOW	NACHHOLEN NACHLAUFEN	make up (work) run after someone
VOR – BEFORE, AHEAD, FORWARD	VORLESEN VESPIELEN	read out loud play (a film)

WEG - AWAY	WEGWERFEN WEGLAUFEN	throw away run away

Practice A: Conjugate the following verbs:

1. sprechen – to speak
2. laufen – to run
3. sehen – to see
4. fahren- to travel

Practice B: Form sentences using the verbs given below

1. einkaufen
2. haben
3. fahren
4. aufstehen

Answers :

Practice A:

Sprechen:

Pronoun	Conjugation
ich	spreche
du	sprichst
er	spricht
sie	spricht
es	spricht
wir	sprechen
ihr	sprecht

sie	sprechen
Sie	sprechen

Sehen

Subject Pronoun	Conjugation
ich	sehe
du	siehst
er/sie/es	sieht
wir	sehen
ihr	seht
sie	sehen
Sie	sehen

Laufen

Pronoun	Conjugation
ich	laufe
du	läufst
er	läuft
sie	läuft
es	läuft
wir	laufen
ihr	lauft
sie	laufen
Sie	laufen

Fahren

Pronoun	Conjugation
ich	fahre
du	fährst
er	fährt

sie	fährt
es	fährt
wir	fahren
ihr	fahrt
sie	fahren
Sie	fahren

Practice B: Examples given below.

Note: You can form different sentences also

1. Wir kaufen in Bangalore ein.
2. Du hast einen Apfel.
3. Ich fahre jeden Tag nach Pune.
4. Er steht um 6(sechs) Uhr Morgens auf.

Role Play A: Listen to the audio and form sentences of your own

Scan the QR code to play the audio

🔊 Pronunciation Practice:

fahren	to travel
sehen	see
lesen	read
essen	eat
heißen	be called
saufen	drink
stoßen	bump
auf	up,on
ein	in

an	towards
los	Come on
ab	from
fern	remote
zuruck	back
kommen	come
fangen	to catch
raumen	room
abfahren	to depart
aufstehen	to get up
kaufen	to buy
stehen	to stand
einkaufen	to shop
aus	out
mit	with
nach	after
vor	before
weg	away

Professions

Objective: To understand the words and phrases related to professions in German

Concept A: Introduction to Profession

- Der Beruf: profession
- Die Berufe: professions

Some phrases related to profession:

Q: What's your occupation? Q: What do you do for a living? A: I'm a...	F: Was sind Sie von Beruf? F: Was machen Sie beruflich? A: Ich bin...
Q: What's your occupation? A: I'm in insurance. A: I work at a bank.	F: Was machen Sie beruflich? A: Ich bin in der Versicherungsbranche. A: Ich arbeite bei einer Bank.

A: I work at a bookstore.	A: Ich arbeite bei einer Buchhandlung.
Q: What does he/she do for a living? A: He/She runs a small business.	F: Was macht er/sie beruflich? A: Er/Sie führt einen kleinen Betrieb.
Q: What does an auto mechanic do? A: He repairs cars.	F: Was macht ein Automechaniker? A: Er repariert Autos.

The question, "Wo arbeiten Sie?" means "Where do you work?" Your reply may be one of the following.

Concept B: Where do you work?

At Deutsche Bank	bei der Deutschen Bank
at home	zu Hause
at McDonald's	bei McDonald's
at the office	im Büro
in a garage, auto repair shop	in einer/in der Autowerkstatt

in a hospital	in einem/im Krankenhaus/Spital
with a big/small company	bei einem großen/kleinen Unternehmen

Concept C: Applying for a Position

"Applying for a position" in German is the phrase "sich um eine Stelle bewerben." You will find the following words helpful in that particular process.

English	Deutsch
company, firm	die Firma
employer	der Arbeitgeber
employment office	das Arbeitsamt
interview	das Interview
job application	die Bewerbung
I'm applying for a job.	Ich bewerbe mich um eine Stelle/einen Job.
Resume, CV	der Lebenslauf

Concept D: Some list of professions:

English	Deutsch
architect	der Architekt
auto mechanic	der Automechaniker
baker	der Bäcker
bank teller	der Bankangestellte, die Bankangestellte
bricklayer, stone mason	der Maurer
broker stockbroker real estate agent/broker	der Makler der Börsenmakler der Immobilienmakler
bus driver	der Busfahrer
computer programmer	der Programmierer, die Programmiererin
cook, chef	der Koch, der Chefkoch die Köchin, die Chefköchin
doctor, physician	der Arzt, die Ärztin
employee, white-collar worker	der Angestellte, die Angestellte
employee, blue-collar worker	der Arbeiter, die Arbeiterin
IT worker	Angestellte/Angestellter in der Informatik

joiner, cabinetmaker	der Tischler
journalist	der Journalist
musician	der Musiker
nurse	der Krankenpfleger, die Krankenschwester
Photographer	der Fotograf, die Fotografin
secretary	der Sekretär, die Sekretärin
student, pupil (K-12)*	der Schüler, die Schülerin
student (college, univ.)*	der Student, die Studentin
taxi driver	der Taxifahrer
teacher	der Lehrer, die Lehrerin
truck/lorry driver	der Lkw-Fahrer Der Fernfahrer/Brummifahrer
waiter - waitress	der Kellner - die Kellnerin
worker, laborer	der Arbeiter
Cook chef as per English	Der Koch, die Köchin

Practice A: Answer the below questions:

1. What do we call Chef in German?

2. What is Lebenslauf called in English?

3. How will you say "I am applying for a job" in German?

Practice B: Initiate a conversation using the phrases and words related to Beruf

Answers to Practice A:

1. Der Koch

2. Resume

3. Ich bewerbe mich um eine Stelle/einen Job

Scan the QR code to play the audio

🔊 Pronunciation Practice:

Der Beruf	profession
Die Berufe	professions
Was sind Sie von Beruf?	What's your occupation?
Was machen Sie beruflich?	What do you do for a living?
Ich bin...	I'm a...
Ich bin in der Versicherungbranche.	I'm in insurance.
Ich arbeite bei einer Bank.	I work at a bank.
Ich arbeite bei einer Buchhandlung.	I work at a bookstore.
Was macht er/sie beruflich?	What does he/she do for a living?
Er/Sie führt einen kleinen Betrieb.	He/She runs a small business.
Was macht ein Automechaniker?	What does an auto mechanic do?
Er repariert Autos.	He repairs cars.
Wo arbeiten Sie?	Where do you work?
bei der Deutschen Bank	at Deutsche Bank

zu Hause	at home
bei McDonald's	at McDonald's
im Büro	at the office
in einer/in der Autowerkstatt	in a garage, auto repair shop
in einem/im Krankenhaus/Spital	in a hospital
bei einem großen/kleinen Unternehmen	with a big/small company
ich um eine Stelle bewerben	Applying for a position
die Firma	company, firm
der Arbeitgeber	employer
das Arbeitsamt (Web link)	employment office
das Interview	interview
die Bewerbung	job application
Ich bewerbe mich um eine Stelle/einen Job.	I'm applying for a job.
der Lebenslauf	resume, CV
der Architekt	architect
der Automechaniker	auto mechanic
der Bäcker	baker
der Bankangestellte	bank teller

der Maurer	bricklayer, stone mason
der Makler	broker
der Börsenmakler	stock broker
der Immobilienmakler	real estate agent/broker
der Busfahrer	bus driver
die Programmiererin	computer programer
der Koch	cook
der Chefkoch	chef
der Arzt	doctor
die Ärztin	physician
der Angestellte	employee
die Angestellte	white-collar worker
der Arbeiter	employee
die Arbeiterin	blue-collar worker
Angestellter in der Informatik	IT worker
der Tischler	joiner
der Journalist	journalist
der Musiker	musician
der Krankenpfleger	nurse
der Fotograf	photographer

die Fotografin	photographer
der Sekretär	secretary
die Sekretärin	secretary
der Schüler	student
die Schülerin	pupil (K-12)*
die Studentin	student (college, univ.)*
der Taxifahrer	taxi driver
der Lehrer	teacher
die Lehrerin	Teacher
der Lkw-Fahrer	truck/lorry driver
der Fernfahrer/Brummifahrer	Truck driver
der Kellner	waiter - waitress
die Kellnerin	Waitress

Adjectives - Predicative Use

Objective: You will be able to learn adjectives in German.

Concept A: German adjectives

1. neu - new

2. alt - old

3. jung - young

4. gut - good

5. schlecht - bad

6. groß - big

7. klein - small

8. kurz - short

9. lang - long

10. spät - late

11. früh - early

12. schwer - difficult, heavy

13. leicht - light

14. einfach - easy

15. schnell - fast

16. langsam - slow

17. billig - cheap

18. teuer - expensive

19. kalt - cold

20. warm - warm

21. heiß - hot

22. glücklich - happy

23. traurig - sad

24. gesund - healthy

25. krank - sick

26. arm - poor

27. reich - rich

28. schön - beautiful, nice

29. hässlich - ugly

30. richtig-right:

31. falsch - wrong

32. wichtig - important

33. müde - tired

34. langweilig - boring

35. interessant - interesting

Concept B: Difference between predicative and attributive adjectives

NOTE:

Predicative adjectives can either refer to the subject or the object of a sentence.

- Das Haus ist schön. (The house is beautiful.)
- Der Clown ist lustig. (The clown is funny.)
- Das Spiel ist interessant. (The game is interesting.)
- Der Film war langweilig. (The film was boring.)

Practice A: Given below are some adjectives in English. Give their meaning in German.

1) Light (weight)-

2) Important-

3) Hungry-

4) Expensive -

5) Cheap-

6) easy-

7) Rich-

8) Wrong -

9) Cold-

Practice B: Fill in the blanks with the adjective of your choice (numbers, colors, etc.)

1) Der Mann ist -------

2) Ich habe -------- Apfel. (number)

3) Die Frau ist -------

4) Das Wetter ist -------

5) Wir schlafen bis ------- Uhr. (number)

6) Das Auto ist ------- (color)

7) Das Thema ist sehr -------

8) Ich habe ------- Buch.

9) Der Elefant ist ------ (color)

10) Der Kaffee ist -------

11) Du fährst sehr --------

12) Deutsch ist -------(easy/ difficult)

Listening Exercise: Listen to the audio and answer the following questions

Practice C: Using simple sentences, describe the images below

Eg:-Der Mann ist krank. - The Man is sick.

Wir sind gesund. - We are healthy

Beautiful Ugly

Fast Slow

1. Fast	Slow
2. Beautiful	Ugly
3. Heavy	Light
4. Old	Young

Answers to Practice A:

1) Light (weight)- leicht

2) Important- wichtig

3) Hungry- hungrig

4) Expensive - teuer

5) Cheap- billig

6) easy- einfach

7) Rich- reich

8) Wrong - falsch

9) Cold- kalt

Answer to Practice B:

1. Alt - old
2. Einen - one
3. Schön - Beautiful
4. Schlecht - Bad
5. Acht - Eight O'clock
6. Blau - Blue
7. Einfach - Easy

8. Ein - A
9. Schwarz - Black
10. Heiß - Hot
11. Schnell - Fast
12. Schwierig - Difficult

Answer to Practice C.

- Der Mann ist alt.
- Die Kinder sind jung.
- Die Kiste ist leicht.
- Der Junge geht schnell.
- Das Mädchen geht langsam.

Scan the QR code to play the audio

🔊 Pronunciation Practice:

Das Haus ist schön.	The house is beautiful.
Der Clown ist lustig.	The clown is funny
Das Spiel ist interessant.	The game is interesting.
Der Film war langweilig.	The film was boring.
Neu	new
alt	old

jung	young
gut	young
gut	good
Schlecht	bad
groß	big
klein	small
kurz	short
lang	long
spät	late
früh	early
schwer	difficult
Leicht	light
einfach	easy
schnell	fast
langsam	slow
billig	cheap
teuer	expensive
kalt	cold
warm	warm
heiß	hot

glücklich	happy
traurig	sad
gesund	healthy
krank	sick
Arm	poor
Reich	rich
schön	beautiful
richtig	right
falsch	wrong
hässlich	ugly
wichtig	important
müde	tired
langweilig	boring
interessant	interesting

Review 3

Objective: This review is to revise the topics as given below:

- Possessive Pronouns
- Verb Conjugation- regular
- Personal pronoun
- Hobbies
- Irregular and separable verbs conjugation
- Professions
- Adjectives - Predicative use

Concept A: Let us study the below Possessiv Pronomen

POSSESSIVPRONOMEN

	SINGULAR MASKULIN	SINGULAR FEMININ	SINGULAR NEUTRUM	PLURAL MASKULIN, FEMININ, NEUTRUM
ich	mein Stift	meine Tasche	mein Glas	meine Stifte
du	dein Stift	deine Tasche	dein Glas	deine Taschen
er	sein Stift	seine Tasche	sein Glas	seine Gläser
sie	ihr Stift	ihre Tasche	ihr Glas	ihre Stifte
es	sein Stift	seine Tasche	sein Glas	seine Taschen
wir	unser Stift	unsere Tasche	unser Glas	unsere Gläser
ihr	euer Stift	eure Tasche	euer Glas	eure Stifte
sie/Sie	ihr/Ihr Stift	ihre/Ihre Tasche	ihr/Ihr Glas	ihre/Ihre Taschen

Concept B: Verb conjugations- regular and Trennbare Verben:

- Ich -e
- du -st
- er/sie/es -t
- Wir -en-n
- Ihr -t
- sie/Sie -en –n

PREPOSMON/PREFIX (general meaning)	EXAMPLE	ENGLISH
AB- AWAY	ALFAHREN	deport

	ASAGEN	cancel
AN- TOWARDS	ANKOMMEN ANFANGEN	arrive begin
AUF – UP, ON	AUFSTEHEN AUFHÖREN	wake up stop
AUS – OUT, ALSO SUGGESTS COMPLETION	AUSSTEIGNEN AUSSTEHEN	get out of a traini stand somebody
EIN - IN	EINSTEIGNEN EINLADEN	get in (train) Invite
LOS – INDICATES BEGINNING SOMETHING	LOSGEHEN LOSBRECHEN	get started break loose/escape
MIT – WITH, DOING	MITBRINGEN MITLOMMEN	bring along come with
NACH – AFTER, FOLLOW	NACHHOLEN NACHLAUFEN	make up (work) run after someone
VOR – BEFORE, AHEAD, FORWARD	VORLESEN VESPIELEN	read out loud

		play (a film)
WEG - AWAY	WEGWERFEN WEGLAUFEN	throw away run away

Concept C: Personal Pronomen

PERSONAL PRONOUNS		
NOMINATIV	**AKKUSATIV**	**DATIV**
Ich	mich	mir
Du	Dich	dir
Er	Ihn	ihm
sie	Sir	ihr
Es	Es	ihm
Wir	Uns	uns
Ihr	Euch	euch
sie	sie	ihnen
Sie	Sie	Ihnen

Concept D : Let's revise the below adjectives

1. **neu** - new
2. **alt** - old
3. **jung** - young
4. **gut** - good
5. **schlecht** - bad
6. **groß** - big
7. **klein** - small
8. **kurz** - short
9. **lang** - long
10. **spät** - late
11. **früh** - early
12. **schwer** - difficulf, heavy
13. **leicht** - light
14. **einfach** - easy
15. **schnell** - fast
16. **langsam** - slow
17. **billig** - cheap
18. **teuer** - expensive
19. **kalt** - cold
20. **warm** - warm
21. **heiß** - hot
22. **glücklich** - happy
23. **traurig** - sad
24. **gesund** - healthy
25. **krank** - sick
26. **arm** - poor
27. **reich** - rich
28. **schön** - beautiful, nice
29. **hässlich** - ugly
30. **richtig** - right:
31. **falsch** - wrong
32. **wichtig** - important
33. **müde** - tired
34. **langweilig** - boring
35. **interessant** - interesting

Concept E: Check the below image for Hobbies and professions:

1. lesen - reading
2. Musik hören – listen to music
3. Münzen/Briefmarken sammeln – to collect coins and stamps
4. fotografieren – photography

5. Rad fahren – bicycling
6. joggen – jogging
7. malen – painting
8. tanzen – dancing
9. singen – singing
10. Briefmarken sammeln – collecting stamps
11. ein Musikinstrument spielen – to play a musical instrument
12. Zeichnen – drawing/sketching
13. Kalligrafie – Calligraphy
14. Internet surfen – surfing the internet
15. Yoga machen – to do Yoga
16. Aerobic machen – to do aerobics
17. mit Freunde ausgehen – to go out with friends
18. im Garten arbeiten – gardening
19. Schwimmen – swimming
20. Skifahren – skiing
21. Schlittschuh laufen – ice skating
22. Angeln – fishing
23. Stricken – knitting
24. Zeichnen – draw
25. Wandern – hiking

26. Kegeln – bowling
27. Sport treiben – to do sports
28. kochen – cooking
29. backen – baking
30. Fernsehen – watching tv
31. laufen – walking
32. Urlaub machen – holiday

Was machst du in deiner Freizit?	What do you do in your freetime?
Klavier spielen	to play piano
Ich spiele Klavier	I play piano
am Computer	on the computer
Ich gehe	I go
schwimmen	swimming
Ich fabre Rad	I go cycling
Ich höre Musik	I listen to music
Ich sehe fern	I watch TV
Ich lese Bücher	I read books
Zeitschriften	magazines

Ich faulenze	I laze around
Ich besuche freunde	I visit friends
Ich gehe ins Kino	I go to the cinema
Ich reite	I go riding

Matching:
German—Professions

Die Berufe

Draw lines between the German vocabulary words and the matching pictures

der Schauspieler
der Bäcker
der Geschäftsmann
der Koch
der Arzt
der Elektriker
der Bauer
der Fischer
der Frisör
der Anwalt
der Musiker
die Krankenschwester
der Fotograf
der Installateur
der Polizist
der Verkäufer
der Wissenschaftler
der Soldat
der Lehrer
der Kellner

Practice A: Write a paragraph on your hobbies and profession:

Practice B: Write 5 sentences each with trennbare Verben

Answers to practice A:

Meine Hobbys sind Tanzen, Reisen, neue Sprache lernen, Krimis und Mythologische Bücher lesen.

Mein Lieblingshobby ist Tanzen. Ich mag tanzen. Ich glaube, dass Tanzen mir sehr schnell zum Abnehmen hilft.

Ich bin Lehrerin von Beruf und ich arbeite selbstständig.

Answers to practice B:

1. Sie hat erzählt, dass er ein Konzert absagt.
2. Ich schickte dir eine SMS, die nie ankam.
3. Es ist schwer, das Spiel wegzulegen.
4. Geht er ins Kino mit?
5. Er sagt ein Konzert ab.

Travel

Objective:I will be able to understand the vocabulary for 'travel' in German.

Concept A: Modes of Travelling:

- Ich kann Vorbeireisen… (I can travel by….)

Straßen. (Roadways)

Eisenbahnen (Railways)

Mit dem Flugzeug. (By plane)

- Straßen. (Roadways)
- Eisenbahnen (Railways)
- Mit dem Flugzeug. (By plane)

Irregular and seperable verbs conjugation

Concept B: German vocabulary used while travelling

Vocabulary	Pronunciations	Translation
der Bus	dehr Buhs	the bus
das Hotel	days HOH-tehl	the hotel
der Zug	dehr Tsoog	the train
der Sitzplatz	dehr SIHTS - plahts	the seat
der Koffer	dehr KOHF -fehr	the suitcase
der Rucksack	dehr RUHCK- sahck	the backpack
das Gepäck	dash Geh-PAECK	the luggage
die Reise	Dee RIY-suh	the trip, the journey
der Urlaub	dehr OOR-lowb	the vacation
die Sonnenbrille	Dee SOHN-Neha-brill-luh	the sunglasses
die Währung	dee VAEH-ruhng	the currency
die Insel	Dee EEN-sehl	the island
das Meer	days May-ehr	the ocean
der Strand	dehr Strahnd	the beach
das Flugzeug	days FLOOG-zoyg	the plane

die Fahrkarte	dee VAHRT-Jahr-tuh	the ticket
das Flugticket	days FLOOG-thick-eht	the plane ticket
der Flughafen	dehr FLOOG-hah-fehn	the airport

Concept C: Phrases used when travelling:

- Darf ich bitte Ihren **Reisepass**sehen? ("may I see your **passport**please?")
- Könnten Sie bitte mein **Flugticket**für mich ausdrucken? ("Could you please print my **Plane ticket**for me?")
- Mein **Gepäck**ist verloren gegangen. (My **luggage**has gone missing)
- Das **Hotel**ist zehn Meter vom **Strand**entfernt. ("The **Hotel**is ten meters away from the **beach**.")
- Ich gehe mit meiner Familie **zum Picknick.**(I go for picnic with my family)
- Jedes Jahr machen wir eine **Exkursion**von unserer Schule. (Every year we go on a field trip from our school.)

Concept D: Vocabulary on Hotel

- Dusche (f) : shower
- Einzelzimmer (n): single room
- Klimaanlage (f) : air conditioning
- Rezeption (f) : reception Desk
- Schlüssel (m) : key
- das Bett: bed
- die Betttücher: sheets
- das Kissen: pillow

Following phrases can be used while reserving hotels:

- Welches Hotel ist am billigsten? (Which Hotel is the cheapest)

- Wie weit ist das Hotel vom Bahnhof entfernt? (How far is the hotel from station ?)
- Haben sie noch ein Zimmer frei? (Are there rooms available?)
- Bis wann muss man sich abmelden? (What time is the checkout?)
- Ich möchte ein Zimmer mit Dusche. (I'd like a room with a shower.)
- Ich möchte ein Einzelbett. (I'd like a single bed)
- Kann ich bitte noch eine Decke haben? (Can I have another blanket, please?)

Concept E: Other words related to Travel

- reservieren: to reserve
- absagen: cancel
- ankommen: to arrive
- mieten: to rent
- abfahren: leave
- bezahlen: to pay
- abholen: to pick up someone (from airport)

Practice A: Choose the correct answer.

1. Das ist ein…?

a. das Flugzeug. b. der Bus. c. der Zug

2. You stay here while travelling or on holidays.

a. Die Insel. b. der Zug. c. das Hotel

3. We use this word to indicate cheap or low cost.

a. billig. b. mieten. c. absagen

4. All essentials needed for your trip packed together is?

a. die Reisepass. b. das Gepäck. c. die Decke

5. Ticket needed for Aeroplane.

a. Flugticket. b. Reisepass. c. Schlüssel

6. Rooms in the hotels are …?

a. die Betttücher.   b. das Bett.   c. Zimmer

7. Translate in German: To pay

a. Mieten.   b. bezahlen.   c. absagen

8. Strand is known _____ in German.

_____

a. Beach. b. road. c. key

9. You need this when the weather is sunny outside.

a. Jacke. b. Rucksack. c. Sonnenbrille

10. Translate in English: das Flugzeug

a. Aeroplane. b. Airport. c. Airticket

Answer for Practice A

1.a. 2.c. 3.a. 4.b. 5.a. 6.c. 7.b. 8.a. 9.c. 10.a

Scan the QR code to play the audio

🔊 Pronunciation Practice:

der Transport	the transport
der Bus	the bus
der Zug	the train
das Flugzeug	the plane
die Lieferwagen	the delivery truck
die Autofahre	the motorist

das Auto	the car
der Motorroller	the scooter
der Heißluftballon	the hot air balloon
der Hubschrauber	the helicopter
das Fahrrad	the bike
der LKW	the truck
das Boot	the boat
der Flughafen	the airport
das Gate	the gate
die Passkontrolle	the passport control
die Ankunftshalle	the arrival hall
die Abflugs halle	the departure hall
Ich mochte bitte einen Fensterplatz haben.	I would like a window seat, please
Ich mochte bitte einen Gangplatz haben.	I would like an aisle seat, please
Brauche ich ein Visum?	Do I need a visa?
Wie lange ist das Visum gultig?	How long is the visa valid for?
Ist der Flug sehr voll?	Is the flight very busy?
Wie lange ist der Flug?	Is the flight very busy?

Wie lange ist der Flug?	How long is the flight?
Hilfe	Help
Hilf mir	Help me
Konnen Sie mir halfen?	Can you help me?
Ich brauche Hilfe.	I need help
Ich bin in Gefahr.	I am in danger
Es ist ein Notfall.	It's an emergency
das Taxi	Taxi
die Fahrkarte	ticket
die Tagesfahrkare	Day ticket
das Reiseburo	Travel agency
die Bank	Bank
die offentlichen Toiletten	Public bathrooms
das Cafe	Cafe
die Wechselstube	Currency exchange
das Einkaufszentrum	Mall/Shopping centre
die Touristeninformation	Tourist center
die Post	Post office
der Bahnhof	Train station
die Apotheke	Pharmacy

die Kirche	Church
der Markt	Market
die Haltestelle	Bus stop
der Taxistand	Taxi stand

Placement of Verbs

Objective: To be able to use verbs correctly in different types of sentences.

Concept A: Placement and meaning of Modal Verbs

Subject + Modal Verb(conjugated form) + …(remaining part of the sentence) + Main Verb (infinitive form)

Modal Verbs:

There are a small group of verbs in German which are known as modal verbs. They are special because they are almost always used with a second verb, and because they have their own grammar rule.

They are:

- wollen - to want to
- Können - to be ablt to/can
- müssen - to have to/must
- dürfen - to eb allowed to

- sollen - to be supposed to/to ought to

These verbs are all irregular in singular only, and follow a similar pattern.

Concept B: Modal verbs' conjugation

	dürfen	**wollen**	**Können**	**sollen**	**müssen**	**mögen**
Ich	darf	will	kann	soll	muss	mag
Du	darfst	willst	kannst	sollst	musst	magst
Er/Sie/Es	darf	will	kann	soll	muss	mag
wir	dürfen	wollen	können	sollen	müssen	mögen
Ihr	dürft	wollt	könnt	sollt	müsst	mögt
Sie	dürfen	wollen	können	sollen	müssen	mögen

Concept C: Weil (because)

Konjunktion: weil		
	Konjunktion	**Ende**
Ich komme nach Deutschland,	weil ich Freunde in Deutschland	hat
Er ist sauer,	weil er morgen	arbeiten muss.
Er ist fröhlich,	weil sein Freund ihn	abholen
Warum ist er müde?	Weil er die ganze Nacht nicht	geschlafen hat

Practice A: Write the following sentences in German.

Practice with Modal Verbs

Schreib es auf Deutsch.

1) I can speak German.

Example - Ich kann Deutsch sprechen.

2) She has to study today. (heute / studieren)

Example- Sie muss heute studieren.

3) We want to see the game. (das Spiel / sehen)

4) Can you go to the concert. (gehen / zum Konzert- to the concert)

5) I should say hello. (sagen / Hallo)

6) May I go to the library? (zur Bibliothek - to the library / gehen)

Practice B: Form 2-3 simple sentences using 'weil' in German.

Practice C: Finish the sentences using endings of your choice.

Remember the second verb goes to the end in its infintive form!

1. Ich kann.......

2. Ich muß.......

3. Ich darf.......

4. Ich will........

5. Er kann.......

6. Wir müssen......

7. Sie sollen..........

8. Er mag...........

9. Du darfst........

10. Man darf nicht......

Answers:

Practice A:

- Wir wollen das Spiel sehen.
- Kannst du zum Konzert gehen?
- Ich soll Hallo sagen.
- Darf ich in die Bibliothek gehen?

Practice B:

- Ich kann nicht gehen, weil ich arbeiten muss.
- Ich lerne Deutsch, weil ich nach Deutschland fahren muss.
- Der Computer ist kaputt, weil er zu alt ist.
- Wir möchten das Spiel sehen.

Scan the QR code to play the audio

🔊 Pronunciation Practice:

Dürfen	to be allowed to
wollen	to want to
können	to be able to
sollen	to be supposed to
müssen	to have to
mögen	to like
darf	may
darfst	may
dürft	may

will	want
willst	want
wollt	want
kann	can
kannst	can
könnt	can
sollst	should
sollt	should
müss	have to
müsst	have to
mag	like
magst	like
mogt	likes

Sports

Objective: To increase our vocabulary about the different types of sports and also how to talk about it in German.

Concept A: Sports with articles in German

Vocabulary	Pronunciation	Translation
das Tanzen	TAHN-tsehn	the dancing
das Joggen	dahs JOHG-gehn	the jogging
das Laufen	dahs LOW-fehn	the running
Golfen	dahs GOHL-fehn	to play golf
der Fußball	dehr FOOS-bahl	the soccer, also: the football (item)
Fußball spielen	FOOS-bahl SPEE-lehn	to play soccer
der Basketball	dehr BAHS-keht-bahl	the basketball
das Radfahren	dahs RAHD-fah-rehn	the cycling
das	dahs BOH-gehn-shee-	the archery

Bogenschießen	sehn	
das Turnen	dahs TUHR-nehn	the gymnastics
das Skifahren	dahs SKEE-fah-rehn	the skiing
das Snowboarden	dahs SNOV-boar-dehn	the snowboarding
im Fitnessstudio trainieren	ihm FIHT-nes-stoo-dee-oh TRAY-nee-rehn	to exercise at the gym
er Sport	dehr Spohrt	the sport
das Surfen	dahs SURF-ehn	the surfing
das Tauchen	dahs TOW-khehn	the diving
das Segeln	dahs SAY-gehln	the sailing
das Schwimmen	SHVIHM-mehn	the swimming
das Rudern	dahs ROO-dehrn	the rowing
die sportliche Aktivität	dee SPOHRT-lisch-uh AHK-tee-fee-taet	the sporty activity, endeavour

Concept B: Sports with verbs in German.

To do sports	Sport treiben
Golf	Golf spielen
soccer	Fußball spielen
Volleyball	Volleyball spielen
Football	Football spielen
Basketball	Basketball spielen
Baseball	Baseball spielen
Hockey	Eishockey spielen
Tennis	Tennis spielen
Table tennis	Tischtennis spielen

Sentences with Sports:

- Ich mag Tennis spielen
- Ich spiele Tennis gern

Practice A: Given below are some sports activities. Give the name of these sports in German.

1. Football
2. Diving

3. Skiing
4. Swimming
5. Jogging
6. Archery
7. Cycling
8. Gymnastics
9. Rowing

Practice B: Translate the below sentences in German.

1. I jog every day at 7 o'clock.
2. I love swimming in Summer.
3. Football is an important sport.
4. What is your favorite sport?
5. Do you play Table Tennis?
6. Do you like to do sports?

Listening Practice: Listen to the video and tell the sports that are mentioned in their specific order.

Answer to Practice A:

1. Football – Das Fußball
2. Diving – Das Tauchen
3. Skiing – Das Skifahren
4. Swimming – Das Schwimmen
5. Jogging – Das Joggen
6. Archery – Das Bogenschießen
7. Cycling – Das Radfahren
8. Gymnastics - Das Turnen
9. Rowing - Das Rudern

Answer to Practice B:

1. Ich jogge jeden Tag um 7 Uhr.

2. Ich mag schwimmen im Sommer.

3. Fußball ist ein wichtiger Sport.

4. Was ist ihr Lieblingssport?

5. Spielen Sie Tischtennis?

6. Magst du Sport treiben?

Scan the QR code to play the audio

🔊 Pronunciation Practice:

das Tanzen	Dancing
das Joggen	Jogging
das Laufen	Running
das Golfen	To play golf
der Fußball	Soccer ball or Football
Fußball spielen	To play soccer

der Basketball	Basketball
das Radfahren	Cycling
das Bogenschießen	Archery
das Turnen	Gymnastics
das Skifahren	Skiing
das Snowboarden	Snowboarding
im Fitnessstudio trainieren	To exercise at the gym
der Sport	Sport
das Surfen	Surfing
das Tauchen	Diving
das Segeln	Sailing
das Schwimmen	Swimming
das Rudern	Rowing
die sportliche Aktivität	Sport activity
Sport treiben	To practice sports
Golf spielen	Golf
Volleyball spielen	Volleyball
football spielen	Football
basketball spielen	Basketball
baseball spielen	Baseball

Eishockey spielen	Hockey
Tennis spielen	Tennis
Tischtennis spielen	Table tennis
Ich mag Tennis spielen	I like to play tennis
Ich spiele Tennis gern	I like to play tennis

Definite and Indefinite Articles (Bestimmt und Unbestimmt Articles)

Objective:: I will be able to understand the concept of definite and indefinite articles.

Concept A: Concept of definite and indefinite articles for different cases.

The Definite article is used to point out that noun, whose identity is known to the reader. In English, a definite article comprises 'the'. In German, it changes according to the case and gender.

Indefinite articles are used to point out that noun, that is general, or whose identity is not known to the reader. In English, we use 'a' and 'an' for indefinite articles. In German, we use 'ein' and 'kein', which changes according to the case of the sentence. Also in German, each noun has a gender. So the articles are divided according to gender, and are assigned to each noun according to its gender.

1. Nominative is the case used for a sentence, where the noun or pronoun is the subject.

2. Accusative is the case which shows the relationship between the direct object and the verb. It answers the question 'Wen'(who/whom) and 'Was'(what).

3. Dative is the case which shows the indirect object of the verb. The indirect object of the verb is the recipient of the direct object. It answers the question 'Wem'(to whom) and 'Was'(what).

*The extra article 'kein' translates to 'not' in English.

Example-

1. Das Haus ist klein. (The house is small)- Here the 'Haus' is the subject and therefore the case is nominative and the article used is 'das' as the 'haus' is neuter gender.

2. Ich schreibe einen Brief. (I am writing a letter)- Here the letter is the direct object, on which the action is happening, and therefore the case is accusative, and the article used is 'den' as 'Brief' is masculine gender.

The articles are decided on the basis of the gender of the noun and the case, the sentence is following.

Concept B: Bestimmt articles (Definite Articles)

	Masc	Fem	Neuter	Plural
Nominative	der	die	das	die
Accusative	den	die	das	die
Genitive	des	der	des	der
Dative	dem	der	dem	den

Examples-

- Der Apfel ist rot.- The apple is red (Nominative)
- Ich habe die Katze.- I have the cat.(Akkusativ)
- Ich spiele mit der Katze.- I am playing with the cat.(Dative)

For plural, in the nominative case, the article for all plural nouns is DIE.

- Die Autos sind teuer.- The cars are expensive.
- Die Äpfel sind rot.- The apples are red.

- Ich habe die Katzen.- I have the cats.(Akkusativ)
- Ich esse Brot mit den Äpfeln.- I am eating bread with the apples.(Dative)

*In Dative, while using plural form of nouns, we add an extra 'n' at the end of the noun.

Concept C: Unbestimmt articles(Indefinite articles)

	Masc	Fem	Neuter	Plural
Nominative	ein	eine	ein	-
Accusative	einen	eine	ein	-
Genitive	eines	einer	eines	-
Dative	einem	einer	einem	-

Example-

1. Ein Apfel ist rot.- An apple is red. (Nominative)
2. Ich lese eine Zeitung.- I read a newspaper.(Akkusativ)
3. Ich esse Brot mit einem Apfel.- I eat bread with an apple.(Dative)

*The article 'kein' follows the same rule as 'ein' and in plural, it follows the rules of 'bestimmten Artikels'

Practice A: From the below sentences classify the article as Masculine, Feminine, Neutrum

a. Der Computer ist sehr alt

b. Die Tasche ist blau.

c. Das Zimmer ist groß.

d. Die Flasche ist neu.

e. Das Hemd ist schön.

f. Der Hund ist nicht so gut.

g. Der Mann ist glücklich.

h. Die Frau ist freundlich.

Practice B: Form sentences using bestimmt and unbestimmt articles

- einen
- das

Practice C: Explain the difference between nominative and accusative according to what was explained, also, form simple sentences regarding pronouns.

Example:- Ich trinke Tee

Accusative sentence because when asked 'what' to the verb, object is the answer.

Answers:

Practice A:

- der - masculine
- die - feminine
- das - neutral

Practice B:

- Ich habe einen Apfel ---- unbestimmt (einen)
- Das Auto ist rot. ----- bestimmt (Das)

Scan the QR code to play the audio

🔊 Pronunciation Practice:

Bestimmt	Definite articles
Unbestimmt	indefinite articles
Priya ist Arm.	Priya is poor.
Das Haus ist klein.	The House is small
Wir sehen ein Spiel in Stadion (das)	We see that game in the stadium
Sie kaufen eine Tasse (die)	You buy the cup
Ich habe einen Hund (der) und eine Katze (die)	I have that dog and that cat
Wie backen Sie einen Kuche ?(der)	How do you bake the cake?

Ich esse einen Apfel(der)	I eat the apple
Wer ist das?	Who is this?
Das ist Peter.	This is Peter.
Was ist das?	What's this?
Das ist ein Bus.	It's a bus.
Der Apfel ist rot.	the apple is red
Die Katze ist freundlich.	the cat is friendly.
Das Auto ist teuer.	the car is expensive.

Negative Articles

Objective: To understand the negative articles in German language and to use them effectively

Concept A: Kein and nicht both mean negation.

When do we use kein and nicht:

Use "kein" if what you are negating is

- a noun preceded by ein/eine
- a noun not preceded by any article

Use "nicht" if what you are negating is

- a noun preceded by "der/das/die."
- a noun preceded by a "possessive adjective" (e.g. "mein," "dein," etc)

- a proper noun (i.e. a name, usually following "sein" or "heißen")

Concept B: Let us study some examples:

- Ist das ein Porsche? = Nein, das ist kein Porsche
- Hat er Haare? = Nein, er hat keine Haare
- Ist das die Professorin? = Nein, das ist nicht die Professorin
- Ist das Berlin? = Nein, das ist nicht Berlin
- Heißt du Elvis? = Nein, ich heiße nicht Elvis
- Spielst du gern Tennis? = Nein, ich spiele nicht gern Tennis.
-

Concept C: Position of 'Nicht'

The most general rules are:

1. 'Nicht' will precede the specific word that is being negated
2. If there is no specific part of the sentence that is being negated, 'nicht' will come at the end.

1. 'Nicht' when a specific word is being negated:

- Ruft Anna an? = Nein, Anna ruft nicht an.
- Gehst du einkaufen? = Nein, ich gehe nicht einkaufen

2. When no specific part is negated, 'nicht' comes at the end

- Haben Sie den Block? = Nein, ich habe den Block nicht
- Haben Sie die Tasche? = Nein, ich habe die Tasche nicht

Concept D: How to use 'kein'?

'Kein' will be declined like Artikel:

Examples:

- Ein Mann -----> kein Mann
- Einen Mann ----> keinen Mann
- Eine Frau ----> keine Frau
- Ein Kind----> kein Kind
- Blöcke -----> keine Blöcke (plural)

Scan the QR code t

Practice A: Answer the below questions

1. Hast du einen Stuhl?

2. Haben Sie einen Kugelschreiber?
3. Hast du mein Handy gesehen?
4. Hast du eine Tasche?
5. Hat Antonio die Tasche?

Answers to Practice A:

1. Nein, ich habe keinen Stuhl
2. Nein, ich habe keinen Kugelschreiber
3. Nein, ich habe dein Handy nicht gesehen
4. Nein, ich habe keine Tasche
5. Nein, er hat die Tasche nicht.

Practice B: Form sentences using kein and nicht

Scan the QR code to play the audio

🔊 Pronunciation Practice:

Kein	negation
nicht	negation
Das ist ein Porsche	It's a Porsche
Nein, das ist kein Porsche	No, this is not a Porsche
Er hat Haare	He has hair
Nein, er hat keine Haare	No, he has no hair
Ist das die Professorin?	Is that the professor?
Nein, das ist nicht die Professorin	No, that's not the professor
Das ist Berlin	This is Berlin

Nein, das ist nicht Berlin	No, this is not Berlin
Heißt du Elvis?	Is your name Elvis?
Nein, ich heiße nicht Elvis	No, my name is not Elvis
Spielst du gern Tennis?	Do you like playing tennis?
Nein, ich spiele nicht gern Tennis.	No, I don't like playing tennis.
Ruft Anna an?	Is Anna calling?
Nein, Anna ruft nicht an.	No, Anna doesn't call.
Gehst du einkaufen?	Do you go shopping?
Nein, ich gehe nicht einkaufen	No, I don't go shopping
Haben Sie den Block?	Do you have the block?
Nein, ich habe den Block nicht	No, I don't have the block
Haben Sie die Tasche?	Do you have the bag?
Nein, ich habe die Tasche nicht	No, I don't have the bag
Ein Mann	A man
kein Mann	no man
Eine Frau	A woman
keine Frau	no woman
Ein Kind	A child
kein Kind	No child

Blöcke	blocks
keine Blöcke (plural)	no blocks (plural)

Reading and pronouncing words

Class Objective: To be able to read and pronounce words in German.

Concept A: To pronounce places in Germany.

- München
- Bonn
- Leverkusen
- Düsseldorf
- Walldorf
- Wolfsburg
- Stuttgart
- Ludwigshafen
- Bad Homburg
- Frankfurt
- Hannover

- Essen
- Hamburg
- Herzogenaurach
- Heidelberg
- Neubiberg
- Bochum
- Darmstadt
- Köln
- Berlin

Concept B: Read the passage below.

Hanna92:

Ich arbeite viel und mein Beruf ist sehr stressig. Ich muss fit bleiben. Ich gehe zwei- bis dreimal in der Woche ins Fitness-Studio und am Montag gehe ich immer ins Schwimmbad. Aber ich bin auch gern zu Hause. Am Wochenende lade ich Freunde ein. Wir kochen und essen gemeinsam, das macht Spaß. Und dann genieße ich auch Kuchen und andere Süßigkeiten. Lecker!

SuperTom Fitness ...

Ich kann es nicht mehr hören! Fitness-Studios mag ich nicht. Ich mache nicht viel Sport, aber ich bin gerne draußen: im Park oder am See. Das ist doch auch gesund! Im Sommer schwimme ich auch gern. Ich fahre mit dem Fahrrad zur Arbeit, das ist genug Sport. Ich esse kein Fleisch und keine Wurst, aber viel Fisch, Obst und Gemüse. Das schmeckt lecker und mir geht es gut!

Practice A: Hear the audio below and list out what is the train car, row and seat number.

Practice B: Read the passage and answer the following questions

Meine Familie

Ich heiße Marco Sartori. Ich komme aus Italien. Ich lebe mit meiner Familie. Wir wohnen schon zwölf Jahren in Deutschland, in

Düsseldorf. Mein Vater arbeitet hier als Lehrer, meine Mutter ist auch Lehrerin von Beruf.

Ich bin vierzehn Jahre alt. Ich habe zwei Geschwister. Meine Schwester heißt Stella und mein Bruder heißt Claudio. Stella ist fünfzehn. Claudio ist neunzehn Jahre alt. Er arbeitet als Fahrer. Meine Schwester und ich gehen zur Schule. Ich spreche gut Deutsch, aber auch gut Italienisch. Meine Hobbys sind singen und tanzen.

Wortschatz

- Italien: Italy
- schon: already
- arbeitet: works(to work)
- als Lehrer: as a Teacher
- auch: also
- Beruf: Profession
- Fahrer: driver
- sprechen: to speak
- aber: but
- tanzen: to dance

Beantworten Sie die folgende Aufgaben(Answer the following quetions).

1. Woher kommt Marco Sartori?.............................
2. Wo wohnt er?...............................
3. Wie alt ist er?.............................
4. Was ist die Mutter von Marco von Beruf?..........................
5. Hat er Geschwister?.................................
6. Wie heißt die Schwester von Marco?..................................
7. Wie heißt sein Bruder?.........................

Practice C : See the below puzzle and mark familiar words related to months, days and seasons in German.

T	G	S	D	R	A	U	N	A	J	U	N	I	J	M
C	I	E	H	E	R	B	S	T	F	I	B	N	I	S
E	B	P	I	T	Z	M	Ä	R	Z	E	J	G	É	O
M	U	T	U	N	A	E	E	R	R	T	E	A	H	M
M	N	E	S	I	J	I	M	E	E	G	M	T	C	M
Z	U	M	G	W	T	D	B	B	A	R	I	N	O	E
R	F	B	N	A	C	O	G	T	E	E	T	N	W	R

O	E	E	G	I	T	N	S	B	Z	R	T	O	R	R
P	B	R	A	K	I	N	M	S	S	A	W	S	H	A
G	R	Z	O	L	E	E	E	A	G	M	O	N	A	T
N	U	P	H	I	V	R	M	H	U	G	C	H	J	E
W	A	U	D	O	H	S	R	S	C	G	H	J	W	A
I	R	I	N	A	T	T	U	S	N	Q	U	N	G	J
F	T	O	J	A	E	A	P	R	I	L	W	S	N	Í
E	S	U	G	N	E	G	E	E	I	M	A	A	T	N

Woche

Mittwoch

Juni

Jahreszeit

Montag

Dienstag

Sonntag

Oktober

Winter

Freitag

Samstag

Herbst

Monat

März

Frühling

Sommer

Februar

Donnerstag

Juli

Jahr

April

August

Dezember

November

Answers:

Practice A:

Train Car: 1, Row:8, Seat:C

Practice B.

1. Italien
2. Deutschland, in Düsseldorf
3. 14 Jahre alt
4. Lehrerin
5. Ja. Zwei Geschwister
6. Stella
7. Claudio

Review 4

Class Objective: To revise all the concepts taught previously

Practice A: Form sentences using nicht and kein.

- Generally **nicht**goes at the end of the sentence, however, nicht also goes before a specific word which is the subject to be negated, rather than the whole sentence.
- **Kein**is used as an unbestimmt artikel.

Practice B: Form grammatically correct German sentences for the English sentences given below.

- My son wants to go to the cinema.
- When do you have to get up tomorrow?
- You must sleep at 10 o'clock.
- Maria can bake very well.
- When should we come?
- You are not allowed to play today.

Practice C: Type in the modal verbs in the present tense.

- Ich (können) _____ dir helfen.
- Ihr (müssen) _____ noch viel lernen.
- Du (dürfen) ___ heute früher nach Hause gehen.
- Er (wollen) _____ nachher einkaufen gehen.
- Ihr (sollen) _____ eure Hausaufgaben machen.

Answers

Practice A:

- Wir essen den Hamburger nicht. i.e. we don't eat the burger
- Ich esse kein Fleisch. i.e. I don’t eat meat.

Practice B:

- Mein Sohn will ins Kino gehen.
- Wann müssen Sie morgen aufstehen?
- Du musst um zehn Uhr schlafen.
- Maria kann sehr gut backen.
- Wann sollen wir kommen?
- Du darfst heute nicht spielen.

Practice C:

- Kann
- must
- darfst
- will
- sollt

Listening Practice: Listen to the video for more German phrases for travel.

Practice Test 2

Objective: To check the understanding of the participants of the topics covered in the training.

Question 1:

Setzen Sie den passenden Verbbegleiter (Nomen oder Pronomen) ein.

01.	studiert in Köln.	(du / ich / Wir / ihr / euch / Sie)
02.	schreiben morgen ein Diktat.	(ich / das Kind / ihr / Udo und ich)
03.	heißt Karl Ullrich.	(ich / Mein Nachbar / sie / ihr / wir)
04.	hat drei Geschwister.	(du / ihr / Sie / sie / mein / Ich)
05.	machen die Hausaufgaben.	(du / er / sie / ihr / Sie / Du / Ihr)
06.	ist nicht verheiratet.	(ich / Karl / Ihr / wir / Lars und Ute)
07.	arbeitet in Wolfsburg.	(du / Ihr / Wir / Ich / Der Hase)
08.	antwortest Holger nicht.	(Ich / Du / Er / Sie / Es / sie)
09.	brauche viel Geld.	(Sie / Er / Ich / Du / Hans / Wir)
10.	kaufst jeden Tag neue Schuhe.	(Hans / Ich / Du / Sie / Der Mann)

Question 2: Write verb conjugations of the below:

1. Lachen
2. Machen
3. Wohnen
4. Arbeiten

5. Aufstehen

6. Kochen

7. Einsteigen

8. Einkaufen

9. einschließen

Question 3: Use the above verbs and make each sentence each

Question 4: Use the below guidelines and write on any topic of your choice

You should use the below:

1. Possessive pronouns

2. Adjectives

3. Bestimmte und unbestimmte artikel

Question 5: Translate the below to german

1. I do not have the book

2. That is not my book

3. Is that a pen? No, that is not a pen

4. Is it a table? No that is not a table

5. I do not know the lady.

Answers to question 1:

1. Ihr
2. Udo und ich
3. Mein Nachbar
4. sie
5. Sie
6. Karl
7. Ihr
8. Du
9. Ich
10. Du

Answers to question 2:

1. Lachen

Ich lache, du lachst, er/es/sie lacht, wir lachen, ihr lacht, sie/Sie lachen

2. Machen:

Ich mache, du machst, er/es/sie macht, wir machen, ihr macht, sie/Sie machen

3. Wohnen:

Ich wohne, du wohnst, er/es/sie wohnt, wir wohnen, ihr wohnt, sie/Sie wohnen

4. Arbeiten:

Ich arbeite, du arbeitest, er/es/sie arbeitet, ihr arbeitet, sie/Sie arbeiten

5. Kochen:

Ich koche, du kochst, er/es/sie kocht, ihr kocht, sie/Sie arbeiten

6. Aufstehen

Ich stehe auf, du stehst auf, er/es/sie steht auf, wir stehen auf, ihr steht auf, sie/Sie stehen auf

7. Einsteigen:

Ich steige ein, du steigst ein, er/es/sie steigt ein, wir steigen ein, ihr steigt ein, sie/Sie steigen ein

8. Einkaufen:

Ich kaufe ein, du kaufst ein, er/es/sie kauft ein, wir kaufen ein, ihr kaufen ein, sie/Sie kaufen ein

9. Einschließen:

Ich schließe ein, du schließt ein, er/es/sie schließt ein, wir schließen ein, ihr schließt ein, sie/Sie schließen ein

Answers to question 3:

1. Er lacht über meinen Witz.
2. Sie macht die Hausaufgabe.
3. Ich wohne jetzt in Delhi.
4. Ich arbeite von Montag bis Freitag.
5. Meine Mutter hat ein gutes Essen gekocht.
6. Sonntags stehe ich um 10 Uhr auf.
7. Er steige den Bus immer um 6 Uhr ein.

8. Frauen kaufen immer viel ein.

9. Die Frau schließt den Schmuck in der Kassette ein.

Answer to question 4:

Hallo! Ich bin Tom Maier. Ich bin 13 Jahre alt und Schüler. In der Schule mag ich besonders Englisch, Französisch und Sport. Meine Lehrer sind sehr nett. Ich wohne in Stuttgart, Bahnhofstraße 20, 70001 Stuttgart. Ich habe ein Handy! Die Handy-Nummer ist 1234/567890.

Meine Hobbys sind Fußball, Schwimmen und Computerspiele. Mein Vater ist Zahnarzt von Beruf, meine Mutter ist Zahnärztin. Meine Eltern haben eine Zahnarztpraxis in der Königstraße in Stuttgart.

Ich habe einen Bruder und eine Schwester. Mein Bruder ist 20 Jahre alt und möchte auch Zahnarzt werden. Er studiert Zahnmedizin. Meine Schwester möchte Tierärztin werden. Sie studiert noch nicht, denn sie ist erst 16 Jahre alt.

Answers to question 5:

1. Ich habe das Buch nicht.
2. Das ist nicht mein Buch
3. Ist das ein Kugelschreiber? Nein, das ist kein Kugelschreiber
4. Ist das ein Tisch? Nein, das ist kein Tisch
5. Ich kenne die Frau nicht.

www.ingramcontent.com/pod-product-compliance
Lightning Source LLC
LaVergne TN
LVHW090053181026
850499LV00038B/859
9789356100497